W9-BJJ-619

Pregnancy

DISCARDED

Other Books of Related Interest

Teen Decisions Series
Alcohol
Sex
Smoking
Violence

Opposing Viewpoints Series
Abortion
Adoption
Teenage Pregnancy
Teenage Sexuality
Teens at Risk

Current Controversies Series
The Abortion Controversy
Teen Pregnancy and Parenting

Contemporary Issues Companions Series
Teen Pregnancy

At Issue Series
The Ethics of Abortion
Sex Education
Single-Parent Families

Pregnancy

William Dudley, *Book Editor*

David L. Bender, *Publisher*
Bruno Leone, *Executive Editor*
Bonnie Szumski, *Editorial Director*
Stuart B. Miller, *Managing Editor*
James D. Torr, *Series Editor*

Greenhaven Press Inc., San Diego, California

No part of this book may be reproduced or used in any form or by any means, electrical, mechanical, or otherwise, including, but not limited to, photocopy, recording, or any information storage and retrieval system, without prior written permission from the publisher.

Every effort has been made to trace owners of copyrighted material.

Library of Congress Cataloging-in-Publication Data

Pregnancy / William Dudley, book editor.
    p. cm. — (Teen decisions)
    Includes bibliographical references and index.
    ISBN 0-7377-0491-8 (pbk. : alk. paper) —
    ISBN 0-7377-0492-6 (lib. bdg. : alk. paper)
    1. Teenage pregnancy. 2. Pregnancy, adolescent. 3. Youth—
Sexual behavior. I. Dudley, William, 1964–   . II. Series.

RG556.5 .P72 2001
618.2'4'0835—dc21
                                                        00-032162
                                                        CIP

Cover photo: © Will and Deni McIntyre/Photo Researchers, Inc.

©2001 by Greenhaven Press, Inc.
PO Box 289009, San Diego, CA 92198-9009

Printed in the U.S.A.

Contents

Chapter 5: Parenthood

Foreword

The teen years are a time of transition from childhood to adulthood. By age 13, most teenagers have started the process of physical growth and sexual maturation that enables them to produce children of their own. In the United States and other industrialized nations, teens who have entered or completed puberty are still children in the eyes of the law. They remain the responsibility of their parents or guardians and are not expected to make major decisions themselves. In most of the United States, eighteen is the age of legal adulthood. However, in some states, the age of majority is nineteen, and some legal restrictions on adult activities, such as drinking alcohol, extend until age twenty-one.

This prolonged period between the onset of puberty and the achieving of legal adulthood is not just a matter of hormonal and physical change, but a learning process as well. Teens must learn to cope with influences outside the immediate family. For many teens, friends or peer groups become the basis for many of their opinions and actions. In addition, teens are influenced by TV shows, advertising, and music.

The *Teen Decisions* series aims at helping teens make responsible choices. Each book provides readers with thought-provoking advice and information from a variety of perspectives. Most of the articles in these anthologies were originally written for, and in many cases by, teens. Some of the essays focus on ethical and moral dilemmas, while others present pertinent legal and scientific information. Many of the articles tell personal stories about decisions teens have made and how their lives were affected.

One special feature of this series is the "Points of Contention," in which specially paired articles present directly opposing views on controversial topics. Additional features in each book include a listing of organizations to contact for more information, as well as a bibliography to aid readers interested in more information. The *Teen Decisions* series strives to include both trustworthy information and multiple opinions on topics important to teens, while respecting the role teens play in making their own choices.

Introduction

Every day, thousands of women in the United States—including roughly three thousand teenagers—find out they are pregnant. The discovery is truly a life-changing moment. For some women, it is an occasion for joy. For others, including many teens, it is cause for shock and apprehension. Many have experiences similar to those of Amy, a teen who told her story to writer Rebecca Lanning for an article in *Teen* magazine. Amy recalled how she felt when she was sixteen and had been having sex with her boyfriend for a month.

> When my period was late, I took an at-home pregnancy test. Eric was there with me. When we found out it was positive, I absolutely died. I pretty much knew it deep in my heart, but when we saw the results we just sat there and cried. We were both really scared.

For Amy, the positive result on her pregnancy test meant that in a few months, if she did nothing, she would deliver a baby—a person for whom she and the father would be held responsible for supporting and raising. Any plans she had for her future—high school and college education, travel, career, marriage—would be profoundly affected, if not totally disrupted, by that child. Alternatively, she could make plans to give up the baby for adoption, or abort the pregnancy—courses of action that would have their own costs and repercussions.

Thirty or forty years ago, many teens in Amy's situation would have been taken away from school and friends and placed into a special home for young single mothers. They would have been expected to give up the baby for adoption (and never see him or her again). Or if they kept the child, they would have been expected to marry the father, drop out of school, and settle down to become housewives and mothers. Today, pregnant teens have more options. Abortion—once illegal and often dangerous—is now legal. Mothers who give up their children for adoption can have more say in selecting the adoptive parents and staying in touch with their offspring. And single parenthood has lost much of its past stigma and obstacles—many high schools now have day care for student parents, for example. However, the growing array of choices has not necessarily made it easier for teens who find out they are pregnant.

Social Policy Versus Individual Choice

Amy's discovery is repeated nearly a million times a year in the United States. Although teen pregnancy rates in the United States have declined in the 1990s, they remain high compared to other industrialized nations. Most adult leaders view "children having children" as a significant national problem because teen pregnancy is associated with numerous social ills that befall pregnant teens, their children, and society as a whole. Teen mothers are less likely to finish high school and more likely to end up on welfare. Children of teen mothers have lower birth weights, are more likely to perform poorly in school, and more likely to become teen parents themselves. Teen pregnancy has been the focus of numerous social policy debates: Should we teach birth control in sex education classes, or stress abstinence? Should we enforce statutory rape laws more vigorously? Should welfare payments be sharply limited for single teen mothers so the government doesn't "encourage" teen pregnancy?

While the impact of social policy on teen pregnancy is debatable, in the end the prevention and outcomes of teen pregnancy are a result of the choices that teens like Amy make everyday. All teens have decisions to make regarding sex; teens who find themselves pregnant are also faced with profound choices that will probably affect them the rest of their lives.

Teen pregnancy is a sensitive subject that elicits strong emotional reactions—especially from those whose lives are most affected. Polarizing opinions exist on what is the right thing to do. Some people believe that abortion is equivalent to murder, and thus not an option. Some people believe that giving up one's own "flesh and blood" for another family to adopt is similarly unthinkable. Some people believe that marrying at a young age simply because you are pregnant is folly. And some people believe that single teens shouldn't raise children. "Teenagers who get pregnant," writes author Paula Edelson, "are young people who suddenly have to make very grown-up decisions. The choices they face are very complex. No matter what they decide to do, they—and often their families—will always be affected, in one way or the other, by the experience."

Decisions Before Pregnancy

All teens have choices to make that can determine whether or not they or their sexual partner becomes pregnant. One sad fact about the one million annual teen pregnancies in the United States is that most are unplanned "accidents." The possibility of pregnancy—and all the responsibilities that come with it—is something that should be thought through by every teen considering becoming sexually active.

The decision many teens make is to abstain from sex. Many do so because premarital sex runs against their moral or religious beliefs, or to spare themselves from sexually transmitted diseases or the emotional consequences of having sex before they're ready. Others choose abstinence because it is the simplest and the only foolproof way to prevent pregnancy.

Sex education curriculums in many schools stress abstinence and teach how one can say "no" to partners who pressure for sex. Religious organizations such as True Love Waits and secular organizations such as Campaign for Our Children promote abstinence and encourage teens to postpone sex until marriage or until they are older. Surveys of sexually experienced teens find many expressing the wish that they had waited until they were older to have sex. However, teens who choose to forego sex entirely are in the minority. A 1995 study by the U.S. Department of Health and Human Services concluded that slightly more than half of U.S. girls and almost two-thirds of U.S. boys were sexually active by their eighteenth birthday.

For teens who choose to become sexually active (and, except in cases of rape, coercion, or abuse, having sex *is* a choice), pregnancy prevention is still possible. Various medical devices and drugs exist to prevent the fateful encounter of egg and sperm, or prevent the fertilized egg from implanting itself in the woman's uterus. Options range from condoms to birth control pills to injections of Depo Provera or other contraceptive drugs. The effectiveness of available birth control methods varies from 80 percent to more than 99 percent, depending on the method chosen and how faithfully it is implemented. But nothing short of abstinence is 100 percent effective.

Teens today have much more in the way of birth control options and information than teens of previous generations. Contraceptive methods are often openly discussed in high school and middle school sex education classes. Birth control information is readily available on the Internet. Birth control pills and other options are sometimes dispensed at school clinics; where they are not, often teens can obtain birth control information and prescriptions from private clinics.

Yet many sexually active teens fail to take advantage of their access to birth control. The 1995 U.S. Department of Health and Human Services study found that more than one-third of sexually active teenagers did not use any contraceptives during their first sexual encounter. Many sexually active teens use contraception only part of the time or not at all. Amy and her partner fell into this category.

[Eric] promised that I wouldn't get pregnant, nothing would

happen, my parents would never have to know. And so we did
have sex. . . . I was so immature. I had no idea what I was
doing and what risks were involved. He told me everything
would be OK, but in March, about a month after we started
having sex, I was pregnant.

The decision to become sexually involved with someone is
not one that should be taken lightly. If an individual does not
want to become a parent, yet has problems using or even dis-
cussing birth control, he or she is not ready for sex.

Denial and Shame

The thought that "it can't happen to me" that leads many sexually active teens to go without birth control can also play a factor in how teens respond to the reality of becoming pregnant.
One choice that Amy and those in her situation must make is
whether to accept the reality of a positive pregnancy test, or to
pretend it doesn't exist and hope the "problem" will go away. A
surprising number of teens choose the latter course. Girls on
occasion have been taken to the hospital complaining of stomach pains and wound up delivering a surprise baby.

A second early choice facing pregnant teens is what to tell
their parents and family members. Many teens are reluctant to
tell their parents because they don't want to disappoint them, or
feel shame about the pregnancy (and the revelation they were
having sex). Amy's disclosure of her pregnancy brought about
strong disappointment and conflict with her mother and father,
forcing her to eventually move out of the house. However, in
other cases, parents can be surprisingly understanding and supportive once the initial shock has passed. In cases where parents
are less than helpful, an alternative support system should be
found. Amy eventually found a supportive home with her boyfriend's family. Other possibilities include other family members, school counselors, and welfare agencies.

Both denial and shame are believed to be behind the rare,
tragic stories of infant abandonment and infanticide that make

headlines. For example, in 1997 a New Jersey high school student was charged with murder after giving birth to and then strangling a son in a bathroom stall during her senior prom. In November 1999 three men fishing on the Mississippi River found the body of a newborn girl in the cold waters. The Department of Health and Human Services estimates that 105 babies were found abandoned in public places in 1998, 33 of whom were dead or dying (it is unknown how many of them were born of teen mothers). In response, some states have passed laws that allow women to anonymously drop off their newborns at hospitals or firehouses without fear of prosecution.

To avoid such tragedies, pregnant teens need to accept the reality of their situation and confront the choices they face early in their pregnancy. Whatever decision a pregnant woman makes, be it abortion, adoption, or parenthood, time is valuable and delay in making appropriate plans can be harmful. Abortion is safer and less problematic in the early weeks of pregnancy. Adoption can take time to arrange and prepare for. And expectant mothers should begin taking prenatal vitamins and making physician appointments as soon as they find out they are pregnant.

Once a pregnant teen or couple has accepted the reality of their situation, the next step is to consider their options: parenthood, abortion, or adoption. The social circumstances and attitudes surrounding these choices have changed considerably in the past few decades. While teens today have more choices open to them than teens of an earlier era, the choices themselves remain difficult.

Parenthood

The first option Amy considered was parenthood: "At first, Eric and I seriously talked about getting married, getting an apartment, having the fairy-tale life."

Marrying the father and raising the child was a common occurrence among pregnant teenagers of the 1950s and earlier. Lack of a high school diploma or college education was not considered to be a major loss for women expected to be housewives or for men who could find unskilled jobs in agriculture and industry to support their family. In today's society, education is considered key for both men *and* women to ensure their economic self-sufficiency and personal development. The importance of attaining a good education is such that most Americans today do not marry until their midtwenties. It is also one reason that dropping out of school to become a parent is considered a greater social problem than in the past.

Another change in society is the decreased social stigma surrounding single parenthood, since it has become more common. Mothers who never married are now the single largest group of families on welfare. Of the half million teens each year who give birth and decide to raise their children, more than three-quarters remain unmarried.

Decreasing social stigma has not changed that fact that single teen parents face significant financial problems in supporting their children. Teen pregnancy was at the center of welfare reform debates in the 1990s. Critics of government welfare programs—which provide monetary support to mothers with children—argue that they force taxpayers to support what they consider the irresponsible life choices of others. Reforms passed in 1996 require teen parents to live at home or at another adult-supervised household (thus removing any incentive to get pregnant as a way of getting your own apartment) and to remain in school in order to qualify for welfare benefits.

Money is only part of the responsibilities of parenthood. Many teens underestimate how the profound responsibilities of raising a child can totally change their lives. Of course, teens are not alone in this; few adults fully grasp the realities of parenthood before it happens to them. But raising children is a long-term project that is easily one of the most important things people do with their lives, and one that is best met with a certain level of financial stability and emotional maturity.

In evaluating the costs of parenting, both financially and in terms of her future plans, Amy ultimately chose to reject this option:

> I did some checking as to how much it was going to cost in terms of daycare and an apartment. We were both in high school. Neither of us had jobs; we both lived with our parents. Eventually, I realized there was just no way. . . . If I could've raised him on love, I would've done it in a heartbeat. But I know that it takes so much more to make a child happy.

Abortion

Once Amy had rejected parenthood, she considered abortion, "but only for a minute. I knew that that just wasn't something I could do." Although Amy dismissed abortion, that option is chosen by approximately 400,000 pregnant teenagers each year in the United States. It used to be illegal (this didn't stop many teens and other women from relying on illegal abortions, which were often medically substandard and could result in physical injury or death). Since 1973, however, abortion has been a constitutionally protected right in the United States.

Abortion is probably the most controversial of the three options facing pregnant teens. Many people view abortion as murder. Abortion opponents (called "pro-life") argue that in addition to being morally wrong, abortion can cause great harm to women in the form of bodily injuries or stress disorders ("post-abortion syndrome"). People who are "pro-choice" believe it is sometimes the best solution to an unwanted pregnancy. These opposing views color much of what is published and taught about abortion that teens may find as they explore their options. For example, community "crisis pregnancy centers" exist to provide counseling and material and emotional support for pregnant teens—and to dissuade them from having abortions.

Although abortion is legal, some barriers exist for teens. For example, many states have passed laws requiring parental notification or consent for their teenage children to have an abortion.

In addition, the controversy surrounding abortion has caused many people to be reluctant to share their own experiences with it. Thus although abortion is a common procedure that millions of women have used, each pregnant girl or teen couple often seems to face the decision on their own.

Like teen sex, abortion elicits strong opinions on what is morally right and wrong. For teens who are pregnant, the ethical questions surrounding abortion cease to be theoretical as they decide what to do with their lives. In contemplating abortion, teens should be aware that people of both pro-choice and pro-life persuasions agree that abortion is not an easy solution that can simply restore things to as they were before. In addition, most experts agree that it is women who are coerced or feel pressured by others to have an abortion that are most likely to suffer depression, sexual dysfunction, and other psychological problems afterwards. Teens who are considering terminating their pregnancies must confront the moral questions head on in deciding if abortion is the right choice for them.

Adoption

The vast majority of pregnant teens—about 97 percent—choose parenthood or abortion. Those who reject these two options settle on what Amy ultimately decided—having another family adopt the baby.

Adoption, like abortion, has changed in how it works and how it is viewed by society. Prior to the 1970s, adoptions in the United States were "closed" adoptions that were shrouded in secrecy. A primary purpose of adoption was to protect the reputation of the mother and her family from the shame of a birth out of wedlock. Single women who were pregnant were viewed by social workers and others involved in the adoption process as having already made one bad decision (sex outside of marriage) and not being capable of deciding what was best for their child. It was considered harmful for all concerned for the birth mother to get too emotionally attached to the child or involved in the adoption process. Babies were often immediately taken away from mothers after labor and placed in foster care. Sometimes mothers never got a chance to see them or know what gender they were. They were told to put the pregnancy behind them and to avoid all contact with the adoptive family.

Since then the process of adoption has evolved considerably, and pregnant women now have more options regarding how the adoption is performed. In what are known as "open" adoptions, they can choose and meet the adoptive family. They can hold and spend time with the baby after the birth. They can also choose to stay in contact with the child and the adoptive family.

Amy ended up choosing a course that combined elements of open and closed adoptions. The adoption was arranged by the maternity center she resided at during the last four months of her pregnancy. The center gave her three files of prospective adoptive families based on her list of what she wanted for her child. She selected the adoptive family, and met them briefly after the baby's birth. They agreed to exchange occasional pictures and letters. Amy writes:

> I gave them a baby book and asked them to fill it out and send it back to me. After Dillon's first birthday, I got it back. Inside it, they wrote things he'd said and done, and it's really special to me. . . . I also sent them an album of Eric and me. It's full of pictures of us from when we were babies and growing up, so that Dillon will know exactly what we look like. . . . I also wrote him a letter telling him why I did the things that I did and why I made the choice that I did, and I hope he'll always know how much I love him.

Amy chose not to meet Dillon (after the first days of his life) until he reaches the age of twenty-one, at which point, if both of them wish, a reunion can be arranged.

Despite the expanding options concerning adoption, it can remain an emotionally painful choice. Prospective birth mothers often go back and forth on their decision of whether to relinquish their child. Many go through a grieving process after the birth. Others have regrets years later as they wonder what could have been.

Amy eventually graduated high school, attended college, and remained friends with her former boyfriend. She emerged from her pregnancy confident that adoption was the right choice for her. "I knew, without a doubt in my mind, that it was the right decision to make." Amy took several important steps in this decision process. She took a pregnancy test when she suspected being pregnant, told her parents and boyfriend, considered her various options, and made her choice, taking steps along the way to take care of the child growing inside her. She was fortunate in that her boyfriend was with her for the entire process (a father's consent is necessary for adoption).

However, what was correct for Amy and Eric may not be the correct decision for other teens. The stories and articles in *Teen Decisions: Pregnancy* tell of the experiences of teens who made choices similar to Amy's, and those who made very different choices. Chapter One: Choice or Accident? examines the choices teens make *before* pregnancy, including abstinence and birth control, and includes an article about teens who chose to become pregnant and their subsequent experiences. Chapter Two: Decisions About Pregnancy focuses on the critical period right after pregnancy's discovery and the decisions teens immediately face, including whether to inform one's parents. The next three chapters focus on the three primary options for pregnant teens. Chapter Three: Abortion includes both pro-life and pro-choice perspectives. Chapter Four: Adoption describes some of the legal and emotional aspects of this alternative. Finally, Chapter Five: Parenthood briefly describes some of the responsibilities raising a child entails and how particular teens and teen couples are coping with them. It is hoped that this volume will encourage readers to make responsible decisions about pregnancy—including the decision to prevent unwanted pregnancies from ever happening in the first place.

Chapter 1

Choice or Accident?

Questions About Sex and Pregnancy

Portsmouth Better Beginnings Coalition

Many teenagers have misinformed ideas about pregnancy. An example is the erroneous belief that a girl cannot get pregnant the first time she has sex. In an attempt to dispel such myths and to educate teens, the Portsmouth (Virginia) Better Beginnings Coalition was established. The coalition consists of a collective group of teens, parents, community leaders, and health professionals who seek to educate teens about pregnancy prevention. The following questions and answers about sex and pregnancy are excerpted from its website. The first four questions are ones commonly asked by teenagers. The remaining questions were anonymously sent by concerned teens to the website.

---

1. Can I get pregnant the first time I have sex? You can get pregnant the first time, the fifth time, or the tenth time you have sex. It does not matter how many times you have sex, you can still get pregnant.

2. I haven't started having periods yet. Can I have sex without worrying about getting pregnant? No. Because you ovulate before you start your period, you can get pregnant before

Reprinted from "Frequently Asked Questions," Portsmouth Better Beginnings Coalition (www.betterbeginnings.org). Copyright © 1999 Portsmouth Better Beginnings Coalition, Inc. Reprinted with permission.

you ever have your first period.

3. My friend says she only has sex during her period so she can't get pregnant. Does that work? No. You can get pregnant at any time of the month because you can ovulate at any time during your monthly cycle.

4. My boyfriend told me that if he pulls out before he ejaculates, I can't get pregnant. Is that true? No. Some sperm are released before ejaculation—and it only takes one sperm to fertilize an egg.

5. Can you become pregnant if pre-ejaculate comes in contact with the vulva? What is the possibility? Yes, you can get pregnant in this situation. During sexual intercourse, almost all penises pre-ejaculate (leak fluid) before ejaculation. The pre-ejaculate is very concentrated with sperm and nutrients and can easily travel up the vagina and fertilize an egg after it comes in contact with the vulva (genital organs on the outside of a woman's body). The chances of pregnancy are somewhat less than completely unprotected sex; however, it still is a possibility.

6. If my boyfriend and I take a bath together and he ejaculates in the water, can I become pregnant? There is a very small chance you could get pregnant if your boyfriend ejaculates in the water next to you. Certainly, if you are having intercourse or close touching even with penetration in the water there is a real possibility of pregnancy.

> You can get pregnant the first time, the fifth time, or the tenth time you have sex.

7. What is the percentage of teenage mothers who drop out of school? 70% of teen mothers drop out of high school. 40,000 students drop out each year because of pregnancy.

8. What if you are still a virgin, but semen comes in contact with the vulva? Yes, you can still get pregnant even if you have not had actual intercourse (penetration), if semen comes into contact with the vulva or surrounding areas.

9. I had sex with my boyfriend last night and we used a con-

dom, but . . . we found out the condom broke . . . he said we could go get a morning after pill at the local women's clinic but they are closed for the holidays. Will the morning after pill still work if I take it on Monday? And what is the probability of me getting pregnant when it was the 20th day of the 28 day cycle?

"I pulled out of my girlfriend before I ejaculated and we are scared that she is pregnant."

The "morning after pill" should be taken within 72 hours of the incident. There are different regimens which your healthcare provider can prescribe. Also more info can be found at 1-888-NOT2LATE (Emergency Contraception Hotline) or www.not-2-late.com. Also, it is less likely that you'll become pregnant on day 20 of a 28 day cycle, but you can't al-

---

Tips on Abstinence

Abstaining from sexual intercourse is easier than you think! Here are tips that will help:

- *Talk* openly with your partner about your decision to wait. Talking to a parent or other adult can also be helpful in answering your questions and concerns about making the right decisions. Remember adults were once teenagers too.
- Practice using effective *refusal skills:*
  - Use the word NO—there is no good substitute.
  - Use strong *nonverbal* messages—your body language should also say "No!"
  - Repeat the message as much as needed; do not give in!
  - Suggest alternative activities.
  - When appropriate—reject the activity not the person.
- *Goal Setting:* Set realistic long and short-term goals. Stick to your goals! Avoid getting involved in risky things that could interfere with your goals.

Campaign for Our Children, Inc., "What's the 411 About Sex?" Available at cfoc.org/3_teen/3_whats.cfm.

ways count on your menstrual cycle being normal, so it is still a possibility.

10. *I pulled out of my girlfriend before I ejaculated and we are scared that she is pregnant . . . can you tell me how we can find out if she is and what we can do to stop the pregnancy if she is?* There is a chance she could be pregnant, since the pre-ejaculate fluid contains some sperm. If she is not already on birth control, she should start. If she would like "emergency contraception," there are combinations of birth control pills that will cause her to get a period. She can ask a provider at Planned Parenthood or another local family planning clinic.

Birth Control Options

Gary L. Hansen and William W. Mallory

Gary L. Hansen and William W. Mallory, health and so-
ciology educators connected with the University of Kentucky, describe what options exist for teens who do not
wish to become pregnant. The surest method is to not have
sexual intercourse. They argue that if you believe that you
are not ready for sex or that sex outside of marriage is
wrong, you should act accordingly and be firm in saying
"no" to sex. But if you are sexually active or are contemplating having sex, you need to think about birth control
options and discuss them with your partner. Possible birth
control methods include the birth control pill, injected contraceptives, and condoms.

One of the most important choices you will ever make is
when, or if, to become a parent. Since becoming a parent
affects your options in life, you need to ask yourself some difficult questions. What do I really want to accomplish in life?
Would having a child now interfere with my ability to achieve
that goal? Am I really ready to take on the responsibility of raising a child? What support would be available? Could I emotionally and financially handle this situation?

If you decide that you do not want to become a parent at this

Reprinted from Gary L. Hansen and William W. Mallory, "Choices for Controlling
Births," an online article found at www.nnfr.org/adolsex/fact/adolsex_control.html.
Reprinted with permission from Gary L. Hansen.

time, the information contained in this article will provide some of the information that will help you make an informed decision about the strategy for controlling birth that is "best for you."

Since discussions of birth control involve the topics of sex and relationships with intimate partners, many ideas of what is right or wrong and good or bad are involved. Some people's moral and religious values will lead them to view some of the alternatives as being unacceptable. How you view them and whether you practice them is your own personal decision. Being informed about the options will help you decide what you want to do.

Not Having Intercourse Is an Option

The surest way to avoid pregnancy is not to have sexual intercourse. For many unmarried young people, this is the only viable option since they believe either that they are not ready to have intercourse or that sex outside of marriage is wrong. If this describes you, make up your mind to say "no" and stick with it. Remember that acting out your values is a characteristic of sexual integrity.

> One of the most important choices you will ever make is when, or if, to become a parent.

Whether or not abstinence is the best option for other groups of young people depends on a variety of factors such as the nature of their intimate relationships or their marital status.

Despite what you may have heard, everyone is not "doing it." When considering abstinence, it's important to remember that just because you've had sex in the past doesn't mean you have to continue this practice. It's possible to say "no" at any time.

If You Are Sexually Active

If you are sexually active, knowing key facts about the most common methods of contraception can help you make informed decisions. As you consider each method, ask yourself

the following questions:
- Will I have trouble using this method correctly?
- Will I have trouble remembering to use this method?
- Does this method require cooperation from my partner? If so, is that a problem?
- Is this method too expensive?

Thinking about these questions can be confusing and embarrassing. That is normal, but you need to make yourself think about contraception if you are having, or plan to have, intercourse and do not want to become pregnant.

You also need to talk about these issues with your sexual partner. If you don't feel comfortable discussing contraception with your partner, ask yourself, "Should I be having sexual intercourse with someone I cannot talk to?" Contraception works best when a female and male choose and use it together.

The Birth Control Pill. "The pill" is among the safest and most effective forms of contraception for young women. Combination birth control pills, the kind most commonly prescribed, contain two hormones, an estrogen and a progestin. Mini-pills contain progestin only. Both types of pills must be prescribed by a doctor or health care practitioner after a physical exam and risk evaluation.

When using birth control pills, you must take one every single day. It is best if you do this at the same time each day. When used correctly, the pill is a highly effective form of birth control. The lowest expected failure rate is less than 1 pregnancy per 100 users per year. On average, there are about 3 pregnancies per 100 users per year. The mini-pill is slightly less effective.

While the risks from the pill are slight, there are a few side effects like slight weight gain, breast tenderness, and light spotting between your menstrual cycles. In most cases, these are not serious and usually go away. When considering your options, it is important to realize that the pill, or any other form of contraception, is safer than the risks associated with an unplanned pregnancy. The pill does not, however, protect you from sexually transmitted diseases.

Diaphragm or Cervical Cap. The diaphragm and cervical cap are quite similar. A diaphragm is a shallow rubber cup stretched

---

What Teens Say About Avoiding Pregnancy

When it comes to teen pregnancy—why it happens and how to prevent it—teens get loads of advice from adults, but they aren't often asked to offer their own. Along with *Teen People* magazine, the National Campaign to Prevent Teen Pregnancy set out to change this by asking teens directly what they would say to other teens about preventing pregnancy:

1. Thinking "it won't happen to me" is stupid; if you don't protect yourself, it probably will. Sex is serious. Make a plan.
2. Just because you think "everyone is doing it," doesn't mean they are. Some are, some aren't—and some are lying.
3. There are a lot of good reasons to say "no, not yet." Protecting your feelings is one of them.
4. You're in charge of your own life. Don't let anyone pressure you into having sex.
5. You can always say "no"—even if you've said "yes" before.
6. Carrying a condom is just being smart—it doesn't mean you're pushy or easy.
7. If you think birth control "ruins the mood," consider what a pregnancy test will do to it.
8. If you're drunk or high, you can't make good decisions about sex. Don't do something you might not remember or might really regret.
9. Sex won't make him yours, and a baby won't make him stay.
10. Not ready to be someone's father? It's simple: Use protection every time or don't have sex.

"Thinking About the Right-Now," National Campaign to Prevent Teen Pregnancy.

over a flexible ring. A sperm-killing cream or jelly (spermicide) is applied to it and it is inserted into the female's vagina to cover the opening to the uterus (cervix). A cervical cap, on the other hand, is a small thimble-shaped cup made of soft latex rubber that fits over the cervix inside the vagina. It too is used in conjunction with spermicidal jelly or cream. Diaphragms and cervical cups must be fitted by a clinician because women's vaginas vary in size. In addition, if a woman gains or loses considerable weight or gives birth, a refitting is necessary if she is using a diaphragm.

Both devices must be inserted before intercourse and provide protection in two ways. They block sperm from reaching the uterus while the spermicide kills sperm. The diaphragm can be put in the woman's vagina six hours before intercourse and left in for twenty-four hours. The cervical cap can be left in her vagina for up to forty-eight hours. After these devices are removed, they should be cleaned and stored. Directions on how to care for and store them are provided when they are purchased.

The lowest expected failure rate for diaphragms and cervical caps is about 3 to 5 pregnancies per 100 users per year. On average, there are about 18 pregnancies per 100 users per year. Users can get better protection by checking each time they have intercourse to make sure the diaphragm or cap covers the cervix and by having their partner use a condom. Also, reapplying the spermicide for repeated sexual encounters will increase the effectiveness.

Injected Contraceptives

Norplant. Norplant consists of six flexible capsules filled with progesterone that are inserted in a fan-like pattern beneath the skin of a female's upper arm. Once inserted they are only slightly, if at all, visible. A tiny amount of progesterone is released every day and works by inhibiting ovulation, thickening of the cervical mucous, and/or decreasing the thickness of the uterine lining. The procedure for inserting the Norplant device is not painful and can be performed during a 30-minute routine office visit.

Norplant is a very effective means of contraception. The lowest expected failure rate is significantly less than 1 pregnancy per 100 users per year. On average, there is less than 1 pregnancy per 100 users per year. Norplant is effective for five years. At the end of that period, or sooner if the user desires, the Norplant device is removed in a manner similar to that of the insertion procedure. If desired, a new set of capsules may be inserted at the same time the old set is removed.

Steve Kelley. Reprinted by permission of Copley News Service.

Depo Provera Injections. Depo Provera is a contraceptive injection or "shot" of long-acting progestins. Like the pill and Norplant, it keeps a woman's body from producing eggs. A woman using Depo Provera goes to a doctor or clinic to be injected every three months. The first shot is given within the first seven days of a menstrual cycle (within seven days from the first day of bleeding). Since it does not become effective immediately, a woman should use an additional contraceptive method for two weeks after her first injection.

Like Norplant, Depo Provera is very effective. Its lowest expected and actual failure rates are significantly less than 1 pregnancy per 100 users per year. Unlike other hormonal birth control methods, the shot is safe for women who have just had a baby and can be used safely by women who are breast-feeding.

While Depo Provera is a good choice for many women, there are certain women who should not opt for this method. Women who want to become pregnant within the next two years should choose another birth control method since a return to fertility is sometimes delayed.

> You need to make yourself think about contraception if you are having, or plan to have, intercourse and do not want to become pregnant.

Intrauterine Device (IUD). While you may have heard of intrauterine devices, they are not recommended for young women who have never had children. An IUD is usually made of soft flexible plastic in the shape of a "T" and come in various sizes. It is worn inside the uterus after insertion by a doctor or other clinician. While there are a number of theories, we are not completely sure how IUDs work. The lowest expected failure rate is about 1 to 2 pregnancies per 100 users per year. On average, there are about 3 pregnancies per 100 users per year.

Condoms

Male Condoms. The male condom, also called a "rubber" or "prophylactic," is an over-the-counter method used by men. You can buy it without a prescription. It is shaped like the finger of a glove and is made of latex rubber or animal tissue. The condom is rolled onto the erect (hard) penis before the penis comes into any contact with the vagina. It works by catching ejaculated semen (come), thus preventing sperm from getting inside the woman's vagina.

Those using a condom should be careful to leave a little space at the tip to catch the sperm and help prevent it from bursting. The male also should withdraw, while holding the base of the condom, before his erection subsides in order to keep the condom from slipping off. A new condom should be used for each act of intercourse. In addition, avoid storing condoms in warm places and using Vaseline or petroleum-based lubricants that weaken latex.

The male condom's lowest expected failure rate is about 2 pregnancies per 100 couples using condoms per year. On average, there are about 12 pregnancies per 100 couples per year. When used in conjunction with a vaginal spermicide, such as a jelly or foam, failure rates are significantly lower.

Use of latex condoms by those who are sexually active is the most effective way to prevent the spread of sexually transmitted diseases, including AIDS. Using a spermicide containing Nonoxynol-9 along with a condom results in even safer sex.

Female Condoms. One of the newer over-the-counter birth control methods is the female condom. Made of polyurethane, which is a thin plastic, it covers the cervix and the vagina. There are flexible rings both at the opening and at the bottom of the device. The closed end is inserted near the cervix while the outer ring stays outside the vagina and holds the condom open.

The female condom works by catching the male's semen as he ejaculates (comes). It can be inserted up to eight hours before intercourse and is usable during a woman's period. Each condom should be used only once. The lowest expected failure rate is about 5 pregnancies per 100 users per year. On average, there are about 21 pregnancies per 100 users annually. Using the female condom helps prevent sexually transmitted diseases, including AIDS.

Other Methods

Spermicides. Other over-the-counter birth control methods for women include contraceptive foams, creams, jellies, suppositories, films and sponges. All contain chemicals called "spermicides" and are inserted deep into the female's vagina before sexual intercourse. They work by blocking the entrance to the uterus and killing sperm.

Foams, which come in aerosol cans, and creams and jellies, which come in tubes, have plastic applicators. Suppositories and film are inserted by hand. Sponges come in one size and are made of polyurethane foam which contains the spermicide. They must be moistened with water before use and also are inserted by hand. Sponges have a nylon loop so they can be easily removed.

These methods are not as reliable as medical methods but they are easy to obtain and use. Some offer some protection against certain sexually transmitted diseases. Their lowest expected failure rate is about 3 to 5 pregnancies per 100 users per year. On average, there are about 18 to 21 pregnancies per 100 users per year. However, if the female's partner also uses a condom, failure rates are significantly lower.

Fertility Awareness. Fertility awareness, also called "natural family planning" or "rhythm method," is not very effective with young people. The female attempts to pinpoint the days of the month when she is fertile. She monitors daily changes in her body temperature, vaginal discharge, and/or keeps track of her menstrual periods on a calendar. This information is used to pinpoint which days she is most likely to get pregnant. Couples then can avoid intercourse during that time.

The lowest expected failure rate for fertility awareness is 2 to 10 pregnancies per 100 women per year. On average, there are about 24 pregnancies per 100 women per year.

> There are many wide-spread myths about sexuality that result in people relying on methods to control births that simply don't work.

While fertility awareness has no health risks or side effects, it is among the least effective methods of contraception. If your moral or religious values make this the only acceptable method for you to use, however, realize that it is more likely to work if careful records are kept and if both partners have a high degree of self-control.

Methods That Don't Work

There are many wide-spread myths about sexuality that result in people relying on methods to control births that simply don't work. Ineffective methods include:

- douching after intercourse (no matter what you choose as a douche);
- having sex while menstruating;
- having sex in a standing, sitting or other varied position; and
- withdrawal (male withdraws penis from female's vagina before he ejaculates or "comes").

Making Your Choice

It should be obvious by now that there are many choices for controlling births. The first decision you have to make is whether or not you are going to have sexual intercourse. If you decide not to, you don't have to worry about controlling births. If, on the other hand, you are sexually active and don't want to become a parent, you need to practice one or more of the contraceptive methods discussed in this article.

Deciding which method or methods to use is not easy. While some of the methods like condoms, contraceptive foams, creams, jellies, suppositories and sponges do not require you to see a medical professional and are readily available in local stores, some of the most effective methods must be either prescribed or fitted by a medically qualified person. Therefore, it's a good idea to talk with someone trained in helping others make contraceptive choices. Visit your private doctor, your county health department's family planning clinic, or a Planned Parenthood affiliate. These caring medical professionals can help you make the type of informed, responsible choice that characterizes those who act with sexual integrity.

Pregnant on Purpose

Allison Bell

While the majority of teen pregnancies in the United States are accidental or unintentional, some are planned. Allison Bell, a writer for *Teen* magazine, examines why some teens get pregnant on purpose and describes how having a baby affected their lives. Many teens have romantic ideas of being a mother, while others view pregnancy as a way of keeping their boyfriends (a tactic that often does not work). Many see pregnancy and motherhood as their best option in life. But Bell writes that even though schools and government programs are often supportive of teen mothers, the reality of parenting seldom lives up to people's rosy expectations.

Sandra spent her days flipping burgers at a local restaurant, and her nights changing diapers and washing bottles.

We hear a lot about girls who accidentally become pregnant, but you might be surprised to learn some teen moms actually plan their pregnancies. Considering how tough it is to be a teen mother, it's hard to imagine that any girl would choose to be one, but some do. Why? What motivates them? Would they do it again after discovering what life with a baby is like?

Sandra Lucero was just 13—some would say a baby herself—when she first fantasized about having a child. She got kind of

Reprinted from Allison Bell, "Pregnant on Purpose," *Teen*, August 1997. Reprinted with permission from *Teen*.

obsessed with the idea, and even started faking it. "I'd tell people, 'I'm pregnant'; and they'd get all excited and say, 'Gosh, how many months are you?'" the 19-year-old from Anaheim Hills, California, recalls. She'd bask in the attention—until it was evident her tummy wasn't getting any bigger. Then she'd tell everyone the pregnancy test was wrong.

> Considering how tough it is to be a teen mother, it's hard to imagine that any girl would choose to be one, but some do.

Three years later, however, Sandra did become pregnant—for real—through unprotected sex with her boyfriend, who was four years older. While getting pregnant wasn't something she'd actually sat down and discussed with him, in the back of her mind Sandra hoped it would happen. "I was feeling so insecure about everything, I thought being pregnant and having a cute little baby to hold would make me feel better," she says.

After dropping out of school, Sandra thought she'd spend her time blissing out, awaiting the child she hoped would give her life meaning. But in reality she moved into a cramped apartment with her boyfriend—and his mom—where she mostly did a whole lot of nothing. Soon, Sandra started to feel fat, ugly, and, despite the close quarters, terribly alone and unloved. "It wasn't the way it was supposed to be," she says.

Planned Parenthood

A lot of teens get pregnant by mistake, and they make up the majority of teen moms. Out of the almost 1 million teenage girls who become pregnant each year, 85 percent don't plan their pregnancy, according to The Alan Guttmacher Institute, a non-profit reproductive health corporation in New York that tracks teen pregnancy trends. As for the other 15 percent, those pregnancies are intentional.

Maybe girls who get pregnant on purpose don't do their research. For one thing, teen moms often receive poor prenatal care and they face higher complications. Babies born to young mothers are prone to low birth weight and other health problems. Plus, about a third of teen moms live in poverty—and even if they finish high school, they're less likely to go to college or get a good job.

Yet even if they have a clue that motherhood can be tough, some girls go for it anyway; perhaps their romantic ideas outweigh the real-life rigors. "There are girls motivated by the idea that having a baby will give them the love or sense of hope they feel is missing," says Donna Butts, executive director of the National Organization on Adolescent Pregnancy, Parenting and Prevention (NOAPPP) in Washington, D.C. "And some view having a baby as an insurance policy on keeping their boyfriends."

Although that tactic rarely works—ironically, Butts says, most of the fathers check out shortly after the baby arrives—Sandra bought into the idea.

Sweet 16 and Married

Teen pregnancy cuts across all cultures and economic lines. Seventy-six percent of teen pregnancies occur outside wedlock, but the other 24 percent of teen moms are married. Often, these girls see marriage and babies as their only option in life. Many teens become pregnant to feel validated, says Regina Law, young parents program coordinator for Friends of the Family, a nonprofit counseling agency in Van Nuys, California. "I see girls 14 or 16 who are either married or living with their boyfriends—they see getting pregnant as the next logical step."

May—who asked that her last name not be used—is one example. She was 16, the daughter of strict Chinese parents, when she fell for a 26-year-old Vietnamese guy. Her parents disapproved not of his age but of his nationality; they wanted May to marry Chinese. So, partly to get her parents to accept

> Often, these girls see marriage and babies as their only option in life.

him, May and her boyfriend of only five months decided to have a baby.

Their plan worked. Once she was pregnant, May's parents agreed to let her marry her boyfriend (in most states, minors need parental permission to marry). May quit school and moved in with her new husband.

Pregnancy Perks

Could it be that girls who want babies feel freer to do so today than in the past? In general, it seems that being an "unwed mother" is less of a taboo in society's eyes than it used to be.

At some schools, it's considered cool to be 16 with a bulging belly. Take the small, middle-class town of Tipton, Indiana. "Teen pregnancy is not looked poorly upon by peers here," says William Stone, M.D., an obstetrician who cofounded Teen Pregnancy Coalition to help stem the rising teen pregnancy rate in his town. "In fact, it's greeted with a great deal of excitement."

Schools have become much more teen-mother friendly, too. Some offer on-campus day care centers, lifesavers for teen moms who might otherwise have to drop out of school to care for their children. Some people argue, however, that these high-school day care centers are sending the wrong message to teens—that they encourage young girls to get pregnant. "There is this mixed message that the community is sending," Stone says.

> At some schools, it's considered cool to be 16 with a bulging belly.

Schools aren't the only institutions providing aid for young moms: If a girl is on welfare, the government also lends a hand. "There are many programs that take good care of teen mothers—but the down side is, it makes getting pregnant almost look attractive," says Priscilla Hurley, executive director of Teen Awareness Inc./Choices, a Fullerton, California–based sexuality instruction program that emphasizes personal responsibility and abstinence. One attractive parenting program in Hurley's area is Cal-Learn. As long as the girl is getting high school credit, the program pays for day care, mileage for school and job-training travel, books and uniforms. Pama Tavernier, an Orange County social worker with the program, has seen Cal-Learn turn girls' lives around, but even she wonders if the perks may give girls "an incentive to get pregnant."

Surprisingly, the incentive also comes from parents. "Usually the girl's mother is young herself, so she's happy to accept a baby in her life, allowing her daughter to continue her social and school activities," Stone says.

Baby Reality Bites

While girls may plan pregnancies with high hopes, reality seldom matches the fantasy. In fact, Sandra felt so isolated that she followed her boyfriend everywhere—even into the bathroom. In her ninth month, "he asked me to leave," Sandra says. She went home to her parents and had her son. At first, Sandra spent her days flipping burgers at a local restaurant, and her nights changing diapers and washing bottles. Now she lives in an apartment with a roommate and barely gets by on the meager payments from Aid to Families with Dependent Children (AFDC). Although she's gone back to school, Sandra wonders if she and her 2-year-old son will survive until she's able to bring home a bigger paycheck.

> While girls may plan pregnancies with high hopes, reality seldom matches the fantasy.

It's been just slightly easier for May, who now has two sons. She and her husband are still together and they're both attending school and looking forward to the day when they won't have to rely on federal assistance. "It's been a rough time," she says. "If I had to do it over again, I'd take it a lot more slowly."

Christine's Story

Jeanne Marie Laskas

Christine is a middle-class teen from a Chicago suburb who became pregnant. A broken condom was the explanation, but freelance writer Jeanne Marie Laskas, who profiled Christine, suggests that becoming pregnant seemed to fill an emotional need for her. The stories of Christine and those like her demonstrate to Laskas that many teens do not fully comprehend how pregnancy will change their lives and the lives of their families.

Christine Dubin, who at 16 is some six months pregnant, is in English class taking a quiz on *My Antonia* and the Puritan work ethic. Christine knows she will probably flunk this quiz; she was once an A student, but that was back in grade school. In high school the best she could manage were C's. Ever since the pregnancy, though, some of those grades have plummeted to F's. Even so, Christine will tell you she loves school. "I'm just not good at it," she says. She is a religious girl who participates in her church's youth group activities and sings alongside her mom in the Sunday choir.

Teen Pregnancy in Middle America

Christine [is a] junior at Elk Grove High School. A tidy suburb 25 miles northwest of downtown Chicago, Elk Grove is about as

Excerpted from Jeanne Marie Laskas, "Someone to Love," *Good Housekeeping*, August 1996. Reprinted with permission from the author.

Middle America as Middle America gets: The student body is predominantly white, middle class, and scores above average on the ACTs.

Some 100 Elk Grove girls get pregnant each year, a statistic that also makes this school average. Every minute of every day, nearly two teenage girls in the United States become pregnant. That's 114 an hour, 2,740 a day, or one million pregnancies a year. The percentage of first births to unmarried teenagers has increased dramatically since the early 1960's—from 33 percent to 81 percent—according to The Alan Guttmacher Institute (AGI).

You could say that kids having kids doesn't make any sense, given the amount of information teens get nowadays about how to avoid pregnancy, the availability of birth control, and the bleak outlook that remains a secret to no one. Although about 70 percent of teenage mothers eventually go on to complete high school, they are more likely to be poor in adulthood compared to women who have children after age 19.

> Every minute of every day, nearly two teenage girls in the United States become pregnant.

It's a problem that parents and policy makers want to find easy solutions for. We pass out condoms or attempt to enforce abstinence, believing that girls who become pregnant are simply girls who can't control their impulses, watch too much MTV, or are pressured by peers or the media to become sexually active. But step into [their] lives and you see that these girls are not simply young and impressionable. They are not young and dumb. They are not young and lustful. It would seem, instead, that they are young and lost. . . .

Christine's Hopes for the Future

"I am so happy about being pregnant," says Christine. She is a plain girl, with glasses and thin brown hair. She is learning to speak Japanese and even traveled on a school-sponsored exchange trip to Japan last year. "I just can't wait to deliver this baby so I can hold it and play with it," she says.

She plans to marry Mark, the baby's father. "Mark and I can already picture ourselves," she says. "A little house. Decorating our own Christmas tree. It's really visual for us. We can see everything that is going to happen. We just want to, like, be happy. And we realize that we will have to work and everything, but we'll still be able to do fun things. So I couldn't be any happier."

Teenage Pregnancy Rates, Birthrates, and Abortion Rates

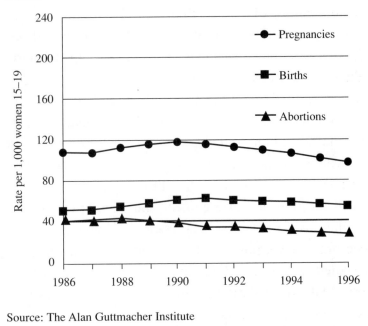

Source: The Alan Guttmacher Institute

Christine has no career goals. She used to think about going to college. "But I'm not good enough for college," she will tell you. "There is no way I could get into college. And now that there is the baby, college doesn't matter at all." On average, only 5 percent of teen mothers ever get college degrees, compared with 47 percent of those who have children at 25 or older.

Counselors who work with teens today see a distinct lack of

goals among the kids. "What's the point of delayed gratification?" says Reverend James Paul Thompson, the associate pastor of the Northwest Evangelical Covenant Church, where Christine sings in the choir. He runs the church's youth group, which Christine participates in. "It's like, 'Why wait until Christmas to open your gifts? Get it now, get it while you can.' That's the attitude. There's an undercurrent that the future is totally uncertain. No security, no security, no security. That is the one thing you consistently hear from these kids."

For Christine, it would seem that her pregnancy has provided her with what she believes to be a haven in an increasingly frightening world. Christine's high school teachers describe her as "a needy girl." The kind that always has a boyfriend—and a boyfriend crisis. Her dependent nature also helped her fit the profile of a girl likely to become pregnant.

The way Christine got together with the father of her child is hardly the stuff of Disney movies. At a heavy metal concert, she got whiplash from throwing herself into the "mosh pit," a crowd of kids dancing crazily and bouncing off one another. The next day, Phil, her boyfriend at the time, picked her up during an argument and shook her. Mark, Phil's best friend, pushed him away from Christine. "And Phil started yelling, so Mark punched him. So Mark and I started getting closer after that."

> For Christine, it would seem that her pregnancy has provided her with what she believes to be a haven in an increasingly frightening world.

Mark had already graduated from Elk Grove; he was a college boy, home for the summer. They dated. They had sex. "But only twice," says Christine. "And the condom broke." The broken condom is the single most common explanation given by the girls in District 214 who end up pregnant.

Christine saw nothing wrong with having sex before she was married. She was in love. And if you are in love, you have sex;

it was her understanding of the way the world worked.

Christine will also tell you that she never concerned herself with AIDS or other sexually transmitted diseases (STDs). "I've never heard anyone talk about AIDS. I don't know anyone who has AIDS," she says. "I know some people in the city do, but not around here." And yet the subject of STDs and AIDS is taught at Elk Grove.

More Contradictions

There are more contradictions. There is the matter of sin. Having been raised in an evangelical Christian family, Christine nonetheless pleads innocent to breaking the rules of her church by having sex before marriage. "It's not immoral to have sex before marriage in our church," says Christine. "In our church, they have you read the Scripture and then you can interpret it the way you want to."

"Huh?" responds Thompson. "We talk about chastity before marriage as God's plan. We talk about right and wrong. She would have been taught that. Quite explicitly." Thompson says it would not be possible for Christine to have misinterpreted these teachings, although it would certainly be possible for a scared teenager to temporarily revise her understanding of sin in the face of anguish.

And then there is the matter of Christine's parents. According to Christine, they are dealing with this pregnancy as if it were a gift from the sky. "They're really happy about it," says Christine. "Everybody is really excited and really happy."

And yet, when Christine broke the news to her parents at school in the presence of two pastors and two counselors—her parents had no idea what the meeting was about when it was called—her father turned white and the school nurse was summoned; his blood pressure had shot up 20 points. Her mother was too busy worrying about her husband's health to even deal with the news of her daughter's pregnancy. Both say they have since calmed down and are facing the situation as a family crisis.

There is, finally, Christine's view of her own future. She does not think it will be compromised by the fact that she will now be faced with the task of raising a child. "I have done everything I wanted to do," she says. "I wanted to try mountain climbing and white-water rafting, and I've done that. I wanted to go to Japan. And I've done that. So I've pretty much done everything I wanted to do. And anything I still want to do, my mom said she would baby-sit. So I don't see how I'm missing out on anything."

Reality Sets In

"Reality for these girls begins to set in somewhere around six weeks after giving birth, and it really sets in around six months later," says [high school counselor Mary Ann] Jahrling. "Because then, no one is stopping by anymore with a present, and no one's fawning over you and your child, and friends have gone on with their lives. And most of the boys—by the time the baby is a year old—they're not around any-more, either.". . .

Counselors like Jahrling and church leaders like Thompson, as well as public-policy makers across the country, are left frustrated by the knowledge that well-intentioned efforts to stem the rate of teen pregnancy seem to have had little effect. Neither the conservative "just say no to sex" nor the liberal "just use a condom" message appears to be working. Maybe the messages are wrong, or maybe the medium is.

> Christine's mother . . . has committed herself to supporting the young couple. . . . Yet she cannot talk about the subject without weeping.

More than half of all teenage families live in poverty—compared to only 14.5 percent of the total population. Women who had babies as teenagers make up nearly half of the welfare caseload.

Jahrling says she has seen a definite attitude shift when it comes to public assistance. It used to be a last resort. "Now it's a right," she says. "It's, 'Okay, fine. If I don't go on my parents' insurance, I'll just go on public aid.' It's an attitude that 'somebody has to take care of me.'"

Echoes Thompson: "They all want to be treated as adults on the one hand, and on the other they want to be taken care of. You want to say, 'Okay, you get a job, you finish school, you take care of the baby, you pay rent, you pay your kid's way.' No way. They say, 'My dad has insurance and my dad has a credit card.'"

Family Support and Grief

Christine's parents both work fulltime outside the home. But her father, a self-employed optician who makes his own hours, has agreed to stay with the baby in the morning while Christine is finishing high school. Does Christine worry about inconveniencing him? She does not seem to understand the question. "He's really happy to do it," she says.

"I'm getting used to it" is the best Christine's father can muster. "I'll see how used to it I am when the baby starts crying in the middle of the night."

Christine's younger brother, Eric, was moved out of his bedroom and into the basement so the baby could have a room. "Eric is really happy about it," says Christine. "Everybody is. Everybody just wishes Mark could be here."

Well, not everybody. Mark's parents, both Polish immigrants and devout Catholics, have refused to let Mark stay over. "They're extremely strict and overprotective," says Mark. "They don't understand."

"They tell me I've ruined Mark's life," says Christine. "And that I've ruined my life. But we don't see it that way."

As for Christine's mother, she has committed herself to supporting the young couple. "You get strong," she says. "You get supportive. You do not get angry. There is no room for anger. This is a quiet house. There is no arguing here." Yet she cannot talk about the subject without weeping. . . .

Epilogue

Christine delivered Angelica Mercedes, seven pounds seven ounces, by induced labor, on February 23, 1996. Two days later, she and Mark were married in a rushed ceremony encouraged by Mark's parents and arranged by Christine's parents. Mark dropped out of college and moved in with Christine's family, taking computer classes at night and working at a computer store by day. Christine took advantage of the tutor Elk Grove provided, but when that was over, she found it was too much to go back to classes and dropped out. She talks about perhaps finishing up at night school next year. Marriage is "fine," although she and Mark are beginning to argue about money. "He won't let me buy anything, but he wants me to pay the bills," she says. "And I have no money at all."

Christine thinks it's important to arrange "at least one hour a week away from Mark." She says motherhood, too, is difficult. "There are times I just sit here and cry because I am not ready for it. Angelica just cries so much. It's real hard to calm her down and keep me calm. Between her and Mark, and our parents, and plus I'm supposed to keep the house clean and cook dinner, it's . . . difficult."

Point of Contention: Is Pregnancy a Responsible Choice for Some Teens?

|Teen pregnancy is associated with many social problems, including poverty, crime, and welfare dependency.| Most American political leaders have decried teen pregnancy, and key aspects of welfare reform passed by Congress in 1996 were meant to make pregnancy and single parenthood less attractive for teens. For example, one provision of the new welfare reforms requires unmarried parents under eighteen to continue their education and live with their parents or in another adult-supervised home. However, some researchers have questioned whether teen pregnancy is truly to blame for poverty and other problems. In this view, teen pregnancy is a result of poverty and other social problems, and teen mothers have become scapegoats, unfairly blamed for a variety of social ills. They argue that pregnancy may actually improve the lives of some teens. The two articles featured here present differing opinions on whether teen pregnancy is a cause or result of poverty and other problems. Kathleen Sylvester is vice president for domestic policy for the Progressive Policy Institute based in Washington, D.C. Kim Phillips-Fein is a feminist writer.

Teen Pregnancy Harms Society

Kathleen Sylvester

All across America, young girls who still are children themselves are bearing children of their own. It is a calamity for these young mothers, because early motherhood denies them opportunities and choices; for their offspring, because most will grow up poor and without a father; and for the nation, because these youngsters are likely to repeat the tragic cycle of poverty and dysfunction into which they were born. However, it is a calamity that is preventable.

Compelling evidence now supports what most Americans long have understood intuitively. Family structure and lifestyle, as well as economics, influence how children turn out. Those of young, unmarried mothers fare badly, and society pays the cost. The equation is straightforward: As poverty is the most accurate predictor of teen pregnancy, teen pregnancy is a near certain predictor of poverty. Two-thirds of never-married mothers raise their kids in poverty.

Children of unmarried teen mothers are far more likely than those of older, two-parent families to fall behind and drop out of school, get into trouble with the law, abuse drugs and join gangs, have children of their own out of wedlock, and become dependent on welfare.

A Critical Situation

The situation is urgent. There are over 9,000,000 youngsters living in welfare families. As they reach adolescence, many are "scripted" to repeat the lives of their parents. It is vital to intervene and break the cycle before those children, too, become parents too soon and create a new generation of disadvantage.

To reverse this cycle requires a categorical declaration by civic, moral, and community leaders that it is wrong—not simply foolish or impractical—for women and men to make babies they cannot support emotionally and financially. It also is time to challenge the complacent view that having babies out of wedlock is simply a lifestyle choice, and that since all such preferences are equally valid, no behavior should be condemned. This stance is untenable in the face of compelling evidence that not all choices are equal in terms of their impact on youngsters, and that children need fathers as well as mothers. . . .

> Children of unmarried teen mothers are far more likely . . . to fall behind and drop out of school [and] get into trouble with the law.

The pattern of life for a poor young woman who becomes pregnant and has a child is predictable. She is likely to have one more child—usually within two years. If she has a second child, she is less likely to finish high school, unlikely to marry, and is at great risk of cycling in and out of the welfare system for a significant portion of her life.

Social Costs
The social costs for offspring of teen mothers also are apparent. Compared to those living in two-parent families, children in single-parent households score worse on measures of health, education, and emotional and behavioral adjustment. Later on, if they continue to live with never-married single parents, they become more likely to drop out of school, become heads of single-parent families themselves, and experience a lower socioeconomic status as adults.

Youngsters who grow up in single-parent households are

at much greater risk of drug and alcohol abuse, mental illness, suicide, poor educational performance, and criminality, according to the National Commission on Children. Two-thirds of the occupants of juvenile detention centers are young men who grew up without fathers, many of whom already have sired children who will grow up without fathers as well. Such consequences are not hard to comprehend. It is difficult to socialize the next generation in neighborhoods where a new generation is born every 14 years.

Any public campaign against teen pregnancy should emphasize how costly it is for all citizens to ignore the situation. The Center for Population Options estimates that 53% of outlays for Aid to Families with Dependent Children (AFDC), food stamps, and Medicaid are attributable to households begun by teen births. Medical services for teen mothers and their kids are especially costly. Young, poor, unmarried, uneducated, and uninsured mothers are much less likely than older, more stable mothers to obtain prenatal care. Pregnant teens frequently deny their pregnancies in the early stages and have poor access to medical services.

Infants born to younger women are more likely to be born prematurely, die in the neonatal period, and be of low birth weight. Each low-birth weight baby averages $20,000 in hospital costs; total lifetime medical expenses for such children can average $400,000. . . .

No Instant Solution

Two messages must be conveyed to young people simultaneously. First, the younger teens should abstain from sex until they are mature enough to understand the consequences of their actions and make informed decisions. Second, when teens are old enough to make that choice, they must do so responsibly. They must not endanger their own health and the health of their partners with unprotected sex, unwanted pregnancies, or unnecessary abortions. . . .

There is no instant solution that will reduce the 80–90% teenage pregnancy rates in America's inner cities overnight. A social change that took decades to become a crisis cannot be eradicated in a year or two. However, the trend can—and must—be reversed.

Each strategy employed may have only a small effect— reducing teenage pregnancy by a percentage point or two a year. Yet, each percentage point represents an enormous achievement. It signifies progress toward a society that values its children. The problem is not insoluble, and there is no time to waste in addressing it.

Excerpted from Kathleen Sylvester, "Preventable Calamity: How to Reduce Teen Pregnancy," *USA Today*, March 1997. Copyright © 1997 by the Society for the Advancement of Education. Reprinted with permission from *USA Today* Magazine.

Pregnancy Improves Some Teens' Lives

Kim Phillips-Fein

Everybody loves a teenage mother. Whether firebrand conservative or bleeding-heart liberal, if you've got a typewriter and a pose to strike quickly, she's your gal. . . . A *Newsweek* cover story summed up what everybody knows about teen motherhood: "The Name of the Game is Shame."

Studying Cause and Effect

A study done by University of Chicago Professor Joseph Hotz may force the moralizers to do some rethinking. In the public debate on teen motherhood, the causal relationship between early childbearing and low income is taken to be axiomatic. Teen mothers stay poor because they're "kids having kids"; with the proper self-esteem classes and a couple of condoms, or lectures on abstinence from a stern patriarch, they'd be sure to be living better lives. It's true that teen mothers are, on average, poorer and have lower levels of educational achievement than the general population. But correlation is not causation, as the statisticians say. Do women become poor because they have children as teenagers? Or do they have children as teenagers because they're poor?

In order to test whether convincing teenage mothers to delay birth will actually improve their educational achievements and income levels, Hotz designed a model that would isolate the variable of pregnancy, showing what would happen to a woman in all other respects similar to a teen mother—except that she had not given birth as a teenager. He analyzed data from the National Longitudinal Study of Youth (a project started in 1979 that interviews groups of teenagers on an annual basis throughout their lifetimes), using as the control group teenagers who become pregnant but miscarry, and then wait to have their first child between ages 20 and 25. These are women who behave the way they would if we had a perfectly designed, perfectly targeted program to stop teen pregnancy, a program that brought the teen birthrate down to zero. But compared to this control group, teenage mothers actually achieve higher levels of economic success: They earn more money and work more hours than they would have had they waited to have children.

> Given the employment prospects for many poor women, [pregnancy] can be a rational response to a difficult situation.

Hotz's study found teen mothers to be, predictably, less likely to work long hours during their teenage years, when their children are young. But once they hit their 20s, teenage mothers work roughly 1,000 hours a year—approximately 100 to 200 hours a year more than they would have if they had delayed childbearing. . . . Teenage motherhood has a similar effect on earnings. Early childbearing initially depresses the labor market earnings of teenage mothers by about $2,500 a year. However, by the time these women reach their 20s, they are earning approximately $5,000 more than they would have if they had delayed their childbearing. According to Hotz teenage mothers earn an average of $11,000 a year at 25 and $19,000 at 30—insufficient salaries for raising a family decently, but not exactly scraping change from the gutter, either. The kinds of jobs low-income women frequently hold—as secretaries, nurse's aides, telephone receptionists—value seniority and experience over credentials. Interrupting a service-sector job to take care of young children is more harmful to mothers' salaries than taking time off from high school is.

No Bed of Roses

Hotz's study leaves plenty of room for naysayers who want to remind us of the obvious—that teenage motherhood is no bed of roses. While they're likely to obtain a GED in their late teens or 20s, teenage mothers are less likely to ever finish high school than those who wait to have kids. Women who bear children extremely young, under age 15, suffer much more severe setbacks in the labor market.

In a perfect world, reproductive freedom wouldn't mean only the power to protect oneself from unplanned pregnancy, but access to the resources that make it possible for a woman to raise a child at whatever point in her life cycle she deems best. But in the world we live in, not even the first condition fully applies. Teen pregnancy can't be ascribed merely to accidents or bad planning, let alone some cultural pathology haunting us from the days of slavery; given the employment prospects for many poor women, it can be a rational response to a difficult situation. As for the problems of the inner city, there isn't any secret formula that accounts for them all—if we want to do something about falling wages and failing schools, we need to talk about the economy and the educational system, and leave the teen mothers alone.

Reprinted from Kim Phillips-Fein, "Taking the Heat Off Teen Moms," *In These Times*, March 4, 1996. Reprinted with permission from *In These Times*.

Chapter 2

Decisions Concerning Pregnancy

The Three Basic Options for Pregnant Women

Planned Parenthood of Houston and Southeast Texas

Women of all ages experiencing an unplanned pregnancy face important choices on whether to choose parenthood, adoption, or abortion. They need to carefully think through their decision and consider each possibility. Planned Parenthood of Houston and Southeast Texas, the publisher of the following brief guide to choosing between parenthood, adoption, and abortion, is part of Planned Parenthood, a nationwide network of medical clinics that provide medical, counseling, and educational services (including abortions) relating to reproductive and sexual health.

A re You Pregnant?
   Maybe you missed a period or feel sick in the morning. Maybe your breasts are tender or you have to urinate frequently. These may be signs of pregnancy. As soon as you suspect that you might be pregnant, make an appointment for a pregnancy test and a pelvic exam. You need to know for sure if you are pregnant.

Reprinted from "Choices," Planned Parenthood of Houston and Southeast Texas (www.pphouston.org). Reprinted with permission.

A urine pregnancy test may give a positive result as early as a few days after a missed period. A pelvic exam should also be done to feel for changes in your uterus that indicate a pregnancy. After a pelvic exam, you will know for sure if you are pregnant and how many weeks you have been pregnant.

> Many women of all ages and backgrounds have had to make the difficult choice between parenthood, adoption, and abortion.

If you are facing an unplanned pregnancy, you may feel alone, scared, angry, guilty, or confused at a time when an important decision must be made.

Many women of all ages and backgrounds have had to make the difficult choice between parenthood, adoption, and abortion. Knowing yourself, being honest with yourself, and remaining true to your own standards will help you make the most responsible decision. It is true that only you can decide what is right for you, but it may be helpful to talk things over with someone you trust . . . a family member, partner, or a friend, or someone in the clergy. One of our brochures offers some thoughts to people who are thinking through their choices. . . .

Parenthood

Parenthood *may be right if* . . .

- I believe I am ready to assume the responsibility of being a parent.
- I can accept the physical and emotional aspects of pregnancy, delivery, and child care.
- I have considered the feelings of my partner and my family.
- I am willing to support my child, and consider my child's needs for the next 18 years.
- I can arrange the necessary finances for this child: medical care, food, clothing, housing, etc.
- I will learn and practice parenting skills.
- I have discussed my need for support with those who care

about me: my partner, my family, or my friends.

- I have considered the possibility that I may have to raise the child alone.
- I am prepared to handle the emotional aspects of parenting.

Adoption and Abortion

Adoption *may be right if . . .*

- I believe I should continue this pregnancy but cannot raise a child at this time.
- I believe this child will have a chance for a better life in another family.
- I am willing to get good medical care, go through labor, delivery and make adoption arrangements.
- I have considered the feelings of my partner and will inform

Teen Pregnancy Outcomes

Miscarriage
(14%)

Birth
(56%)

Abortion
(30%)

More than half (56%) of the 905,000 teenage pregnancies in 1996 ended in births (⅔ of which were unplanned).

Source: The Alan Guttmacher Institute

him of his legal rights.
- I can accept the probability of never seeing this child again.
- I realize there is a possibility that this child may re-enter my life at a later time.
- I am prepared to handle the emotional aspects of adoption.

Abortion *may be right if . . .*
- I believe that I have a right to choose abortion.
- I am choosing out of thoughtful consideration of my circumstances and feelings.
- I have considered the feelings of my partner and my family.
- I can manage the finances of a legal abortion.
- I am willing to make arrangements for the abortion.
- I am prepared to handle the emotional aspects of abortion.

Making Your Choice

Take into consideration your feelings as well as facts when you consider how this pregnancy will affect your life situation now and in the future. The choice is yours, but that doesn't mean you must be alone in making your decision.

Seek out the people who will support you: your partner, family, friends, clergy, or a professional counselor.

The staff of Planned Parenthood can help answer your questions about health care costs, health risks, parenting, adoption facilities, and abortion.

When Do You Have to Decide?

You should begin prenatal care or have an abortion *early* in your pregnancy. If you think you may be pregnant, whatever choice you make, you should call your clinic right away. If you choose to have an abortion, the procedure can be done as soon as a pregnancy test is positive.

Telling Your Parents

Melissa DeMeo

Many teens faced with an unwanted pregnancy may be reluctant to tell their parents. As this article by Melissa DeMeo from the *Brown University Child and Adolescent Behavior Letter* explains, however, teen pregnancy is often a time of crisis, and one that teens should not face alone. Parents may be more understanding and supportive than you may think.

You're probably scared. You're probably anxious. Maybe you feel guilty, or betrayed, or even, despite it all, a little happy. Or maybe you're so overwhelmed, you don't feel much of anything.

Pregnancy, planned or not, at whatever age, is always a time of crisis. Crisis in the original sense of the word—a decisive point in someone's life. This is a decisive point in your life, and you've already taken a good first step by talking it over with someone.

You should consider also telling one or both of your parents. That may not be feasible if you know your parents would hurt you, or throw you out of the house. If, on the other hand, you come from a family that's usually been supportive in the past, they may be a source of support and advice right now, at a time when you could really use it. In fact, a lot of pregnant teens tell their parents—almost three out of four.

Reprinted from Melissa DeMeo, "I'm Pregnant: What Am I Going to Do?" *The Brown University Child and Adolescent Behavior Letter*, vol. 13, no. 1, January 1997. Published by Manisses Communications Group, Inc. For more information call Manisses customer service at 1-800-333-7771. Reprinted with permission.

How to Tell Them

OK, so you're gonna tell them, you really are. But not right now, when mom's on her way to work. Or when your little brother is around. Or when your father looks like he's in a bad mood. You can't just march into the kitchen and say, "Guess what? I'm pregnant." Can you?

> If . . . you come from a family that's usually been supportive in the past, they may be a source of support and advice right now.

Pick a time when no one's in a rush to go somewhere, and a place where you feel comfortable and have some privacy. But the only way to say it is to just say it. In plain, simple language.

If you still can't get the words out of your mouth, you could ask your parent (or parents) to go to your counselor's or therapist's office with you, and tell them there, with the help and support of an objective third party. While you've got everyone together, you can also discuss what you're planning to do about your pregnancy.

The scary part is that you won't know how your parents will react. You may think you know them so well that you're sure they're going to be mad, or disappointed, or just totally flip out. And maybe they will. But maybe they'll surprise you.

Have you told your boyfriend? Maybe you both could talk about your options with a counselor. Or, maybe you would prefer to go by yourself.

You Must Decide

Ultimately, no matter who else knows, only you can make the final decision, which might be the scariest thing of all. Some women your age are so frightened by the prospect that they ignore the fact that they're pregnant, pretending that the problem will go away. The irony is that by not making a decision, you actually are deciding to carry the pregnancy to term, whether that's what you really want to do or not.

It's a hard decision to have to make, but it's better to face it

head-on, as soon as you can. Abortions are safer earlier in pregnancy rather than later, should you choose to have one. If you
decide to have a baby, it's best to get prenatal care as early in the
pregnancy as you can.

You have three options. None of them is easy but you do have
options, and you can pick the one that's best for you and everyone else involved:

- Abortion
- Adoption
- Parenting

You may want to get information on all three, and your therapist can point you in the right direction. Ask your doctor (if you
don't have one, you should find one: ask your school nurse, or
call your health insurance plan for a referral). You can go to your
local Planned Parenthood clinic. You can look up "adoption" in
the Yellow Pages.

Not all of this information will be helpful, and, unfortunately,
some of it may be biased. No one knows better than you how
emotionally charged a pregnancy can
be, so consider the source of your information, and try to base your decision on
your values and circumstances—not
someone else's.

When you're faced with a tough decision, everyone tells you to make a list of
the pros and cons, or advantages and
disadvantages, of each option. Some-
times the simple act of seeing things written down may give you
visual evidence of the best path. Similarly, you could keep a
journal of your choices and feelings as a way to figure it out.

> Some women your age are so frightened . . . that they ignore the fact that they're pregnant, pretending that the problem will go away.

No Perfect Solution

You may discover that no decision is ever black and white. If
you're looking for the perfect solution, there isn't one. There's

only the best of a limited number of alternatives. But you can, and will, get through this, and maybe learn something valuable in the process. Like maybe you're really not ready for an intimate relationship. Or maybe you didn't know how to get birth control, or were too embarrassed to ask anyone. Or maybe you thought getting pregnant would keep your boyfriend from breaking up with you, or that having a baby would give you someone to love.

Think about it. Talk to someone about it. This is about you, your health, your family and your future: What could be more important?

Coping with Stress and Taking Control of Your Future

Katherine A. Kelley

Discovering an unplanned pregnancy can be an extremely stressful experience, writes Katherine A. Kelley, nursing director for emergency services at Rideout Memorial Hospital, California. She argues that teens who find themselves in this situation need to take charge of their lives, carefully examine their options, and not let other people make decisions for them. She also offers suggestions on how to inform family and friends and on dealing with stress.

Y ou are sitting in the office of the doctor who has cared for you for many years, or, wanting anonymity, you have gone to someone you've never met. It seems like you have been there forever and you just want to go home and hide from the world. The problem is, you also desperately want to know the answer to the ultimate question: are you pregnant? You sit there, hoping and trying to reassure yourself that it's just some fluke of nature that you haven't had a period for three months. The doctor walks in, looks at you and tells you that you are eight weeks pregnant. Your heart jumps to your throat, your stomach churns and you

Excerpted from Katherine A. Kelley, "You Are Pregnant, Now What?" in *Dear Diary, I'm Pregnant*, edited by Anrenée Englander. Copyright © 1997 Anrenée Englander. Reprinted with permission from Annick Press.

begin to shake all over. Maybe you feel like your whole life is over, but at the same time there might be positive feelings as well. You look down at your stomach and back at the doctor with dozens of questions in your head. Where do you start?

The doctor starts talking about your options, appointments, ultrasounds, health insurance and so on. You don't hear a word because you are immediately worried about what you are going to tell your family and friends and how they will react. You might suddenly feel very alone in the world. As you make your way home, your mind races through the obvious options: you could hide the pregnancy from everyone (but for how long?), or get an abortion immediately (but how and by whom, and how do you pay for it?).

You have just been through one of the most stressful experiences a woman can have. You are faced with hundreds of issues about your life and your pregnancy. The issues are complicated and charged with emotion.

> You can work towards taking charge of your life in a way that you may never have done before.

You can take one of two pathways in handling this situation. One, you can allow people around you to take over your life and get you through this with very little input from you. This would allow them to make decisions that you will have to live with, and possibly regret. This might be a way of avoiding conflict and pressure, but in the long run it may not make you very happy.

Two, you can work towards taking charge of your life in a way that you may never have done before. This will take a lot of strength and courage. It might not be easy. The payoff is that you will make decisions that—as much as possible—will meet your needs rather than other people's. They will be decisions that you feel you can live with. You will gradually feel stronger and have better self-esteem as a result of learning to take control: the more you do it the more you will have. Also, if you decide to continue with your pregnancy, making your own choices will probably give your child the best chance for happiness.

Getting Help—the Next Step

First, you need to get reliable information, and as soon as possible. Once you have decided whether you will continue with your pregnancy, you will have to act quickly, but right now you need to give yourself time to think and to get the best information available to help you make your choice. There are several ways to do this. The telephone book is an excellent place to start. An organization called Planned Parenthood has offices in many communities and offers cost-free, valuable information and counselling services. Some branches have health-care professionals who will do most tests and examinations for free. Women's clinics and crisis clinics are also good places to call. There are other organizations and clinics listed that offer counselling for pregnant teens, but evaluate these carefully. Some of them have hidden biases and try to persuade teens to make one particular kind of decision about their pregnancy. It is extremely important that you keep this fact in mind: nobody should give you advice about which choice to make. If you are talking to someone who makes you feel guilty or pressured, or even just uncomfortable, find another organization. Libraries and women's bookstores have information on local clinics and counselling services too.

Another source of information might be your school nurse or family doctor. You should be aware, though, that even health-care professionals sometimes have unsympathetic reactions to pregnant teenagers and might be unsupportive. Try not to let this upset you too much. These attitudes are their problem, and should not be made into yours as well. . . .

Examining Your Options

Making your decision will be extremely emotional. At the same time, it is one that should be made with intelligence and a full understanding of the consequences. It requires you to take into consideration the plans you have for your own life. If you possibly can, try to get some counselling from a professional health-care worker (like a doctor or nurse), clinic or public health organization. They will give you information and talk with you about each of your options: abortion, adoption or motherhood.

It is important to remember that it's natural to have second thoughts, whatever your final decision. This is a very complicated choice to make, and many teens feel insecure or confused if they have mixed feelings. Don't expect a perfect decision from yourself; there is no such thing. If you have carefully thought through your choice, you will probably identify it as the best choice possible for you under the circumstances. . . .

What Do I Tell My Parents?

This might depend partly on what decision you make about your pregnancy. Some teens who choose abortion decide not to tell their parents, fearing a hostile reaction.

If you decide to tell them about your pregnancy, try to think through ahead of time what you want to say and what the facts are. Talk it over with someone you trust, whether a friend, counsellor, spiritual leader, partner or someone else. If you are especially nervous, it might be a good idea to have another person with you, someone who is sympathetic to you and can offer you support during the family discussion. Ask that person ahead of time, tell them what you want to talk about and give them time to decide. If one person says no, don't get discouraged—find another one. Some organizations offer counselling services involving parents. There may be a health-care professional, teacher or sports coach who would be willing to be present when you talk to your parents.

Your parents might not react the way you expect—positively or negatively. You might be nervous, but what you don't need to be is ashamed. You have not committed a crime. What has happened has happened and cannot be reversed; therefore, it is important to move on and make decisions about the future.

Your parents might want to dwell on the "horrible mistake you've made." They might want to say "I told you so." They

Calculate Your LMP

Whatever you decide to do about your pregnancy, you will need to know the first day of your last menstrual period, or LMP. This is the "start date" of your pregnancy, even though conception probably occurred sometime after this period. This date is used to predict your due date, or when and how an abortion may be performed. If you are not sure, then figure out the range of time within which your last period began—for example, "sometime in March" or "after December 15 when school got out but before Christmas."

If your last period was unusual, especially if it was light and came at an odd time, be sure to note this and be sure to tell your doctor or the clinic staff when discussing your LMP. An unusual period could mean you were pregnant *before* your last period. This is critical information when considering an abortion. When you visit a doctor or clinic, staff can use ultrasound imaging to determine just how far along your pregnancy is.

If there is any chance that you will continue your pregnancy, you should begin prenatal care—a regular program of medical care during your pregnancy—within ten weeks of your LMP.

Elective abortion (that which is not medically necessary) is accessible up until about twenty-six weeks (or six months). If you choose abortion, however, it is much better physically, financially, and (many people feel) ethically to have it within the first twelve weeks. Later abortions are hard to obtain in some areas, as well.

When you call a clinic or doctor, they will always ask for your LMP, so memorize it!

Anna Runkle, *In Good Conscience,* 1998.

might feel that it's their right to make the decisions, to control you and the situation. Quite simply, it is not. Your parents' decisions might be based on their need to save face or avoid the neighbours finding out. Remember that, while they might be suffering some embarrassment, you are facing a life-changing event. The consequences are yours alone. Don't misunderstand: your parents are not the villains here, but they have a very different point of view than you do at this time.

Take this time to try and take control of your choices and future. Let your family know that you have given some thought to your options. If possible, involve your partner in this effort.

Coping with Stress

This is, of course, a very stressful time for you, but there are some basic steps that can help you deal with it.

1. Don't make big decisions right away. You are not yet in the frame of mind to think clearly through many of the decisions you will have to make. Make only the simpler ones at this point: choosing what doctor you are going to see, which person or people you want to confide in initially, and so on. (These might not seem like simple decisions, but they are as simple as they get in this situation.) Keep in mind, however, that the decision to end your pregnancy ideally should be made before the twelfth week. Abortions that are done after that point are more complicated.

> Making your decision will be extremely emotional.

2. Find a friend. Someone might surface in your life as your much-needed friend. It might not be who you think it will be. They may not always know what to say or do, but they do want to help. Try not to shut people out because they don't understand what you're going through. Explaining what is happening to you could help them understand, and it might give you a chance to gain new perspectives on things.

3. If possible, talk with the father. Find out what you can expect from him. Let him know that what you need right now is emotional support. Just like you, he is going to find this a very confusing and difficult time. You may need to give him some time to think clearly and offer you the support you need. Don't expect it to happen immediately: it might take a while or, in some cases, never happen at all.

> The fact that you are pregnant doesn't mean that you have to give up all of your dreams for the future.

A man's view of pregnancy is very different from a woman's. His priorities are very different from yours. He is not influenced by the same pressures and emotions that you are in this situation, and he may see things in a strictly practical way. He might, for example, arrive at the idea of abortion before you do. He might feel that this is the only answer at first, and it does not necessarily mean that he doesn't care about you or wants to "get rid of the baby." Explore with him why he feels the way he does and try to understand it. Again, keep in mind that it is your body and ultimately your decision.

Many of us as teenagers have a very hopeful view of our prospects for marriage and family life, even if our family life was far from perfect. Because of this, you might decide that you ought to get married. However, now is not the time to make that decision; it is a big one, and you and your partner need to make it without pregnancy being a factor. Don't pressure him to get married, and resist your parents' pressure as well.

4. Try to avoid confrontations. Talking with friends and relatives may lead to uncomfortable discussions that bring up or intensify long-standing problems in those relationships. If you feel that this is happening, try to get out of the conversation and avoid that person in the future. Become aware of people who put pressure on you or try to control you, and of situations that are uncomfortable in these ways. Avoid them if you can. You might also find counselling helpful in learning coping skills for these and other situations that you may find yourself in.

5. Try to stay on course. The fact that you are pregnant doesn't mean that you have to give up all of your dreams for the future. If anything, you need to become more committed to those dreams. You may have to deal with some delays and/or find another route to achieve your goals, but you are young. You have the strength and courage to achieve them. Avoid any decision that closes doors to opportunities. For example, don't turn down scholarships or admissions to colleges or universities; these things can be postponed for a variety of reasons, and pregnancy can be one of them.

Learning and Growing

Everything in your life has changed, and change can be hard to accept. You might feel older, or find that things that were once very important to you don't somehow seem that important any more. One day you may look around at your friends and suddenly think they seem very young. It may be hard to fit in with your usual friends.

The way you view your parents will change. Your relationship with your partner will undoubtedly change—or might even end. These are things over which you may not have control.

However, you can work on controlling your responses. Try to focus on the aspects that are positive. Perhaps you have found a new friend who understands what you are going through. You might even find that you and your parents become closer. New dreams, just as exciting and fulfilling, might replace the old ones.

Believe in yourself. Because of all you are going through, you are going to grow and learn. You are going to find within yourself more strength than you ever thought possible. Recognize these resources within yourself and take pride in your ability to draw on them.

Nothing in life can give you more satisfaction than making your own choices and finding within yourself the courage to see them through.

Nine Months of Hiding

Katherine DeStefano

Faced with the shock of becoming pregnant, some teens attempt to conceal their predicament. Katherine DeStefano tells how she engaged in self-denial about her pregnancy when she was eighteen, and how she concealed her pregnancy from her family until after the baby was born. She later decided that not telling her parents was a mistake.

I just could not face the reality. It was July 2, just after my last year in high school, and I was looking at the results of a home pregnancy test. It was one of those plus-minus ones, and I just refused to believe it read positive. Then it started to hit me that I really was pregnant. I would just lie in my bed and cry.

I didn't tell anyone but Michael, my boyfriend. I'm the oldest of four kids, and I was worried that this whole situation would make my parents stricter on my brothers and sisters. I thought of abortion, but it just would have been a quick fix, and I couldn't do it. Then I leaned toward adoption, and just not telling anyone it ever happened. But then I felt the baby kick at 4 or 5 months. My boyfriend and I decided we didn't want to spend the rest of our lives wondering if our child was being properly taken care of.

It wasn't hard to conceal that I was pregnant. My belly simply didn't get very big. I'm petite, and I kind of sucked in my stomach as much as I could. It was winter, and I wore spandex

Reprinted from Katherine DeStefano, "Nine Months of Hiding," *Newsweek*, July 7, 1997. Reprinted with permission from the author.

and long sweaters. I knew the baby was going to come, but I put off thinking about it. It's kind of like if you're sick. You know you should see a doctor, but you don't. You say, 'Well, I'll wait and see if it goes away.' But a baby's not going away.

In the last month I got panicky and blocked it out. I would just go to my job at a department store every day. I was lifting heavy boxes, so it's a blessing I had a healthy baby. I also later found out I had pregnancy-induced high blood pressure, which is very dangerous. I didn't go to a doctor until I went into labor; I told my mom I was going to see a doctor because I had a bladder infection. When I came back home, my mother said, "You're pregnant, aren't you?" She had suspected that something was wrong. She said, "Oh, God, you had an abortion—is that where you went?" I said no. She said, "I'm not going to yell." She was so calm. I was shocked. I had thought she would lose it if she ever found out.

> It wasn't hard to conceal that I was pregnant.

I was so relieved. It had been nine months of hiding and torture. Now I realize it was wrong not to tell my parents. Just think—are your parents really going to kill you? They love you. As it turned out, I had the baby that evening, a healthy little girl.

Chapter 3

Abortion

Abortion—A Controversial Solution to Unwanted Pregnancies

David M. O'Brien

Approximately one-third of the pregnant teenagers in the United States choose to terminate their pregnancies before birth. As University of Virginia government professor David M. O'Brien writes, abortion has been legal in all fifty states since a Supreme Court decision in 1973 (*Roe v. Wade*), but it remains a focus of controversy and moral disagreement. O'Brien summarizes some of the arguments for and against abortion and describes some of the methods by which abortions are performed.

A bortion is the ending of a pregnancy before birth. Early in a pregnancy, the fertilized egg that grows and develops is called an *embryo*. After three months of development, it is usually called a *fetus*. An abortion causes the embryo or fetus to die. In a *spontaneous abortion*, also called a *miscarriage*, the fetus passes from the woman's body. Spontaneous abortions may result from such natural causes as an abnormality in the embryo, a hormonal imbalance, a long-term disease, or some other disorder in the

Excerpted from David M. O'Brien, "Abortion," an online article found at www.worldbook.com. Excerpted from *The World Book Encyclopedia*. Copyright © 2000 World Book, Inc. Reprinted with permission from the publisher.

woman. In an *induced abortion,* the fetus is purposely removed from the woman's body. This article deals with induced abortion.

Induced abortion has been a topic of dispute for hundreds of years. People disagree on two basic questions. One question is whether the law should permit a woman to have an abortion and, if so, under what circumstances. The other is whether the law should protect the unborn. Those who wish to legally limit or forbid abortion describe their position as "right-to-life" or "pro-life." Those who believe a woman should have the right to an abortion refer to themselves as "pro-choice."

> Arguments against abortion are generally based on the belief that an abortion is the unjustified killing of an unborn child.

Arguments against abortion are generally based on the belief that an abortion is the unjustified killing of an unborn child. Most people who oppose abortion believe that human life begins as soon as a sperm fertilizes an egg. Some believe that human embryos and fetuses should have legal rights and that abortion is actually a form of murder. Many pro-life people believe that legalization of abortion increases the number of irresponsible pregnancies and leads to a disrespect for human life.

The Roman Catholic Church is probably the leading opponent of abortion. Conservative branches of other religions also disapprove of abortion.

Arguments for Abortion

Many people would allow abortion under certain circumstances. Some approve of abortion if a woman's life or health is endangered by her pregnancy. Others find abortion permissible if medical tests predict that the child will be born with a serious mental or physical defect. Some people would permit abortion when a pregnancy has resulted from rape or incest. Others believe that a woman should have an unrestricted right to an abortion, especially before the fetus becomes *viable*—that is, capable of living outside the mother's body. Most fetuses become viable after the sixth month of the pregnancy.

People who favor an unrestricted right to abortion during early pregnancy often separate human life from *personhood*. They argue that personhood includes an ability to experience self-consciousness and to be accepted as a member of a community. These people believe fetuses are not persons and thus should not be granted the rights given to persons. Such pro-choice thinkers consider birth the beginning of personhood.

Another pro-choice argument is that legal abortion eliminates many of the illegal abortions performed by unskilled individuals under unsanitary conditions. These abortions cause many women permanent injury or result in their deaths. Also, some argue that women should not have to give birth to unwanted children because the world's population is growing rapidly and natural resources are becoming scarce. . . .

Abortion in the United States

Abortion in the United States is a subject of public debate. Opinion polls show that most people think abortion should be legal. These people might disapprove of abortion or disagree with some of the reasons that women seek abortions, but they would permit a legal choice. Some believe only the states—and not the federal government—should regulate or outlaw abortion.

Before the mid-1800's, abortion was not a crime under U.S. common law if it took place before *quickening*. Quickening is the time when the mother first feels the fetus moving. State laws prohibiting abortion began to appear in the 1820's. By 1900, every state except Kentucky had made abortion a serious crime. But some courts refused to impose penalties for early abortion.

By the 1960's, pro-choice organizations in the United States had begun working to change state abortion laws. By the early 1970's, 14 states had laws permitting abortion if the woman's health was in danger or if the woman was a victim of incest or rape.

In 1973, the Supreme Court of the United States delivered a historic decision on abortion in the case of *Roe v. Wade*. The court ruled that states could not forbid a woman to have an abortion during the first *trimester* (three months) of pregnancy. The court based this ruling on the assumption that an early abortion is usually safer for the woman than a pregnancy that lasts a full nine months. The court also ruled that, during the second trimester, states may regulate abortion only to protect women's health. Once the fetus becomes viable in the third trimester, states may regulate abortion to protect the interests of both women and the unborn. The *Roe v. Wade* decision stated that the U.S. Constitution implies the right of privacy and allows a woman to decide for herself if she will have an abortion.

Tony Auth. Copyright © The Philadelphia Inquirer. Reprinted with permission of Universal Press Syndicate. All rights reserved.

The 1973 decision also dealt with the question of when a fetus becomes viable. It stated, "Viability is usually placed at about seven months (28 weeks) but may occur earlier, even at 24 weeks." The court said that states may forbid abortion of a viable fetus except when the abortion is necessary to protect the life or health of the mother.

Since the *Roe v. Wade* decision, many groups have organized in the United States to oppose abortion and the legislation and court decisions that permit it. These groups include the National Right to Life Committee and the Christian Coalition as well as Operation Rescue, which conducts demonstrations near abortion clinics. Most pro-life groups strongly oppose illegal acts. However, some individuals have vandalized, bombed, or set fire to abortion clinics. Others have attacked and killed doctors and other clinic employees.

> People who favor an unrestricted right to abortion during early pregnancy often separate human life from *personhood*.

Pro-choice groups also have expanded their efforts. They contact lawmakers, hold demonstrations, and attack restrictive abortion laws in court. Pro-choice organizations include the National Abortion and Reproductive Rights Action League, the Planned Parenthood Federation of America, and the National Organization for Women. . . .

Abortion in Other Countries

In other countries, abortion laws differ. Lawmakers in some countries have considered abortion an effective tool for limiting family size and combating poverty. In China, for example, abortions are legal and common because the government allows only a limited number of children per family. Chinese women may have an abortion at any time during their pregnancy. In Russia, abortion is allowed up to the 29th week of pregnancy. Japan restricts abortions to the first 24 weeks of pregnancy. Both Russian and Japanese women are allowed to use abortion as a method of birth control.

In the United Kingdom, an abortion may be performed up to the 24th week of pregnancy. However, it must be shown that continuing the pregnancy would endanger the physical or mental health of the woman or her children.

Canadian law permits abortion at any time during pregnancy

and for any reason. However, most physicians avoid performing abortions during the later stages of pregnancy and do not offer abortion as a method of birth control.

Abortion Methods

Physicians perform abortions in several ways. During the first trimester of pregnancy, the most common method is *suction curettage*, also known as *vacuum aspiration*. This method involves removing the fetus by suction, then scraping the woman's uterus with surgical instruments called *curettes*.

Abortion can also be caused in the first trimester by a drug called *mifepristone* or *RU-486*. The drug blocks the action of the hormone *progesterone* in the woman's body. Normally, this hormone prepares the woman's uterus to receive and nourish the embryo.

In the second trimester, many physicians use a method called *dilation and evacuation,* or simply *D and E*. In this method, the fetus is taken apart in the uterus and removed. Another method involves adding a salt solution to the *amniotic fluid,* the liquid that surrounds the fetus. The fetus then dies and passes from the woman's body. A second-trimester abortion also may be performed by adding hormonelike drugs called *prostaglandins* to the amniotic fluid. The drugs cause muscle contractions that expel the fetus.

Some Advice for Teens on Obtaining Abortions

Planned Parenthood Teenwire

What do teenagers need to know if they are thinking about having an abortion? The following advice on what steps to take is furnished by the Planned Parenthood Federation of America, a nationwide network of clinics that provide medical, counseling, and educational services (including abortions) relating to reproductive and sexual health. The federation believes that teens, like all women, should have the right to terminate their pregnancy if that is their decision. It urges teens to carefully consider their options and to seek support from their parents if possible. It also warns against "crisis pregnancy centers" that attempt to frighten women away from abortion.

If you've decided to have an abortion, you probably have a lot of questions. It can be a stressful experience, so you will need to take good care of yourself both physically and emotionally.

Abortion is a touchy subject with a lot of people. Remember that this is your body and your decision, even if your boyfriend or your parents or your friends feel differently. You have a right to end an unwanted pregnancy if you feel that it

Reprinted from "What About Abortion?" an online article found at www.teenwire.com. Copyright © 1999–2000 Planned Parenthood® Federation of America, Inc. Reprinted with permission from *teenwire.com*™. All rights reserved.

is the wisest decision for you.

Here are some next steps that will help you cope.

1. Consider your options carefully and get more information about the procedure.

If you're at all unsure about your decision to have an abortion, think about your options. Planned Parenthood and other family planning clinics have specially trained counselors to talk with you, explain the abortion procedure, and help you sort it all out. Take a few days to be sure, but don't wait too long. Abortion is safer, cheaper, and easier in the first 12 weeks of pregnancy.

Be aware that hundreds of so-called "crisis pregnancy centers" have been established across the country to frighten women away from choosing abortion. Your local Planned Parenthood will be able to direct you to a reputable clinic that will not try to influence your decision one way or another.

2. Find someone to help you.

Being pregnant when you don't want to be can be scary and confusing. Find a person you trust, who can support you and help you get through this. That person could be a parent, your boyfriend, your best friend, your sister—anyone you feel would be right for this situation.

If you don't feel like you have anyone who will understand and be supportive, ask for a counselor at Planned Parenthood. They are specially trained to help you cope—whether or not you have the support of your parents and friends.

If your pregnancy is the result of a rape, you should seek help from a rape crisis center. They will help you get additional counseling and care that you might need, and will talk to you about possibly filling out a police report.

3. If you can, tell your parents.

Although it might be frightening or difficult to tell your parents, they're in the very best position to help you. Most parents care about their kids very much—they want you to be healthy and happy and most of them will put aside their anger or sadness to help you.

Although the procedure itself is safe and fairly easy on your body, it may be uncomfortable and emotionally demanding. You will at least need money ($250 or more) and a ride to and from the clinic at least once. Most women feel enormous relief after an abortion, but even they sometimes find that they need some emotional support—extra hugs, a shoulder to cry on, and some wise words from the people who love you. So unless you believe it will make life truly difficult or put you in danger, it may be

State Parental Consent and Notification Laws as of January 2000

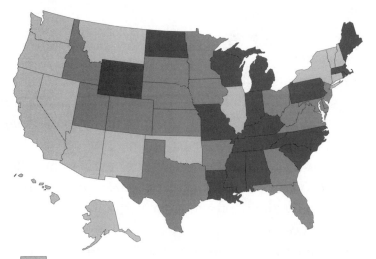

States with no parental involvement requirement

States that require some form of parental or family notification before an abortion can be performed on a minor

States that require some form of parental or family consent before an abortion can be performed on a minor

In most cases, a teen seeking an abortion can bypass parental notification or consent by seeking a hearing from a judge.

Source: Planned Parenthood

best to tell your parents, even if that's hard to do.

4. Learn about your state's laws.

Many states have parental consent or notification laws. Consent laws require that a parent (or both parents) say it's okay for you to get an abortion. Notice laws require that your parent(s) know about your intention to have an abortion in advance. If you don't feel that you can tell your parents, a judge may be able to give you permission to get an abortion anyway. The counselors at the clinic in your area will be able to explain the laws in your state or region of the country and help you make arrangements.

5. Make an appointment with a clinic you trust.

Many Planned Parenthood health centers and other clinics offer abortion services. Call 1-800-230-PLAN to find a Planned Parenthood in your area.

6. Rearrange your schedule to give yourself a few days off after the abortion.

Many women feel physically and emotionally drained for a short time after an abortion. You will have some cramping and bleeding. And along with relief, abortion can bring up temporary, unexpected feelings of anger, regret, guilt, or sadness. If this happens, be gentle with yourself. For most women, these feelings pass quickly, but if they continue, you should see a counselor at your clinic for some follow-up support.

7. Use birth control.

You should always be sure to use birth control so you aren't faced with an unintended pregnancy again. Your abortion provider will be able to help you find condoms, give you a prescription for birth control pills, or discuss other birth control options with you.

Some Reasons to Decide Against Abortion

Monnica Terwilliger

For many people, abortion is the immoral taking of a human life and a choice that should not be considered lightly, if at all. Much of the advice and information pregnant women receive may reflect this fundamental belief. The following selection of responses to possible reasons for abortion is by Monnica Terwilliger, a counselor for the Westside Crisis Pregnancy Center. The center is one of numerous "crisis pregnancy centers" whose purpose is to counsel women against abortion and to provide medical and other support for women who choose not to terminate their pregnancies.

I f you are pregnant and planning an abortion, it's important to evaluate why you are making this decision as well as the consequences to your choice. Below are some of the most common reasons women choose abortion with a response to consider.

My parents will kill me if they find out.

Yes, your parents will be upset and disappointed, but they will probably not kill you. After the initial shock, parents of pregnant young women usually come to terms with the situation, later becoming an invaluable source of support. Usually we see that the

Reprinted from Monnica Terwilliger, "Before You Choose, Consider This," an online article found at www.w-cpc.org/abortion/consider.html. Reprinted with permission from the author.

grandparents-to-be are excited about the baby as the due date approaches. If you are afraid to tell your parents, a counselor from your local pregnancy resource center can work with you to determine the best way to break the news.

If you decide not to tell your parents, our experience has been that the parents usually find out anyway. In these situations, mothers especially are saddened that they weren't given the opportunity to support their daughter when she most needed it.

You don't understand. They'll kick me out of the house!

If your parents really do kick you out, your pregnancy resource center can help you find another place to stay while you are expecting. Some centers have a registry of families who have volunteered to house pregnant girls as needed. There are also many fully equipped maternity homes with young women staying there who are in your same situation. The maternity home will assist you with prenatal care, parenting education, counseling, and many other needs you may have.

> Legally, no one can force you to have an abortion.

My parents are forcing me to have an abortion.

Legally, no one can force you to have an abortion. In fact, forcing a minor to have an abortion is child abuse. If you tell the doctor that someone else is forcing you into this decision, he or she will not perform the abortion.

My boyfriend will leave me if I have this baby.

Your boyfriend is just as responsible for the pregnancy as you are. It takes two to make a baby, so his responsibility does not end just because he doesn't want to deal with the situation anymore. If he is going to leave you just because you want to give your unborn child a chance at life, it's questionable whether he loved you at all. He is treating you as no more than an object for his sexual needs, rather than a woman who is rightfully concerned about the effects of abortion on herself and her child. You may be better off without someone like that in your life right now. Either way, he is still legally required to pay child support after the baby is born.

I'm so embarrassed! What will everyone think?

If you are unmarried, you may fear that others will judge you for having a child out of wedlock. But there are many single parents today, some divorced and some never married. Years ago this was a real concern, but today the stigma attached to single parenthood is far reduced. In fact, many metropolitan school districts, like Los Angeles, include publicly funded high schools especially for pregnant and parenting students.

I've got my whole life ahead of me. A baby doesn't fit into my plans.

If you are ever planning on having children, one thing you will come to understand is that there is usually never an *ideal* time to have a baby. No matter when you decide to have a child there will be trade-offs and sacrifices to make. It's impossible to predict the future. Many couples wait a very long time to start their families, only to find later that their circumstances never became ideal.

I'm not ready to be a mother.

It is true that parenthood requires more responsibility than single life, but if you are pregnant you are already a mother. You are being responsible for the child inside of you by the way you treat your body now. The real question is, "How do I treat this child that I have already participated in creating?"

What's the big deal? It's not a baby yet.

Although the unborn child does not have legal rights under the law, the fetus is very alive. By the sixth week of pregnancy the heart has started beating. By eight weeks brain waves can be measured. By twelve weeks the child can and does cry, though silently. By sixteen weeks the baby's movements can be felt by the mother. Many women bond with their unborn children long before they are born and feel a great sense of loss after an abortion.

I don't want to end up poor and on welfare. I need to finish my education.

Having a baby does not have to mean that you will end up as a welfare mother, even if you are poor and single. Although it may be more difficult to continue your studies while you are caring for an infant, many women complete their educations and go on to have fulfilling and exciting careers even while doubling as mothers. Many find that having a child increases one's motivation to succeed. Organizations like the Nurturing Network (1-800-TNN-4MOM) exist solely to help students and aspiring professional women complete their goals while facing an unplanned pregnancy. Our experience has been that a woman's motivation and self-esteem determine her ability to do well, not an unplanned pregnancy.

> Having a baby does not have to mean that you will end up as a welfare mother.

An abortion seems so much easier than pregnancy. I just want to get this over with.

The abortion procedure is quick, but the effects can last a lifetime. Abortion can leave you emotionally impacted for years. In our experience, common post-abortion symptoms include depression, nightmares, guilt, regret, avoidance of babies, and even self-destructive behaviors. The difficulties usually get worse over time and not better. Most dating relationships do not survive an abortion as the experience drives the couple further apart. Some women are physically damaged from the abortion, and a few are even left permanently infertile. In our center we have spoken to women who have almost bled to death after what was supposed to be a safe, simple procedure. If this is your first pregnancy, aborting can double your risk of developing breast cancer; multiple abortions can increase your risk of breast cancer three-fold.

I don't have any medical insurance.

It's not too late to get coverage for your prenatal care and delivery. Most college students are covered for pregnancy under their university health plans. If you are unemployed, a high-school student, or otherwise have little income, you will most likely qualify for Medi-Cal (a California state program). If you make too much money for Medi-Cal, but not enough for private insurance, you may qualify for AIM—a California state-subsidized plan for low-income women and children. You may even be able to obtain private insurance if you apply early in pregnancy. If you are not a U.S. citizen, there are still some public funds you may be able to access.

I can't afford a baby.

Babies can cost as much as parents are willing to spend. Much of our society focuses on having numerous possessions for ourselves and children, but material things do not create a loving family. After you look back on your life, those things which you value the most will not be the possessions you spent a lot of money on, but rather your children and relationships. It's more important to invest in the new life inside you than all the things you think you and your baby will need.

Having a baby will increase your budget, however, regardless of how thrifty you are. For this reason, most pregnancy resource centers offer maternity clothes, baby clothes, and baby equipment to any woman who needs it at no charge. Programs like WIC [Women, Infants, and Children] help women and their children obtain healthy foods at no cost. Also, you can save a tremendous amount of money by purchasing baby furniture second hand. Relatives are often eager to buy infant clothes and other goods, especially if this is the first baby in the family for a long time.

> The abortion procedure is quick, but the effects can last a lifetime.

The doctor said that there might be something wrong with the baby.

While most prenatal tests can reasonably predict a problem, they don't usually give insight as to the severity of the problem. The problem may be very minor. Sometimes such tests are wrong and the child is completely healthy. And even if the disorder is severe, the value of a human being is not dependent on the health or attractiveness of that individual. Handicapped children deserve a chance at life just as anyone else. A disabled child is still able to love and be loved, and to make a special contribution to your family. Depending on your outlook, this child can be a blessing to you and others. You will probably need support to continue your pregnancy under such circumstances. Call our center for a referral to organizations made up of parents who have continued pregnancies under similar circumstances.

Nonetheless, if you feel unable to raise a child with special needs, there are adoption agencies which can place such children in loving homes. Call a pregnancy resource center near you to discuss your situation.

I just had a baby. I can't have another one right now.

If you have just recently given birth, it can be a tremendous shock to find that you are pregnant again. But having just been pregnant, you can understand more than anyone just how fantastic it is to have a small child developing and growing within you. You've experienced the miracle of life before; to extinguish this life now is hard to imagine. Two babies close together is a real challenge for even the most experienced mother, but in a few years you will find that the siblings are the best of friends. The children will entertain each other giving you more time later on. Having another baby will be invaluable to the child you have now and will soon be precious to you too.

Why I Had an Abortion

Beth Dawes

What is it like to have an abortion? Beth Dawes (a pseudonym) tells her own story of how she opted for abortion, having decided that she was not ready or willing to have a child. She tells how she reacted to finding out she was pregnant and her fears and uncertainties over the abortion procedure. She then describes her trip to the abortion clinic and having the abortion itself. Although she did not relish the experience, she believes that it was the best choice for her.

The EPT test is a plastic rod with two tiny windows in it. I'm supposed to urinate on the end, but I'm afraid I'll miss, so I rinse out an empty cream cheese container and pee in that instead. If I'm pregnant, a pink line will appear in both the round and square windows. If not, only the square window will change. The rod sits on the bathroom countertop primed for action. The instructions say it will take three minutes, but I watch with horror as a pink line appears almost instantly in both windows. I thought I'd prepared myself for the worst, but suddenly I am overwhelmed with panic.

Getting pregnant has always been one of my worst fears, even before I became sexually active. This is partly because I've always known I would have an abortion. My plans for the near future are built around my dreams of becoming an accomplished

Reprinted from Beth Dawes, "I Had an Abortion," *Teen*, February 1997. Reprinted with permission from *Teen*.

professional athlete, not marriage and family. Before my boy-friend Scott and I ever considered having sex together I told him how I felt. I explained that I was in no position emotionally or financially to take on the responsibility having a child. He is young too and has career plans that don't include a family in the near future.

When we finally realized we were at a point where we wanted to become physically intimate, we were extra careful about using condoms and practicing safe sex. We weren't reckless, but we also weren't immune to mistakes. One night a couple months ago when we realized the condom had broken, it was bother-some but soon forgotten. Little did we know that we were about to experience firsthand the alarming difference between dis-cussing abortion and actually having to go through with it.

Sitting there in that bathroom, with the EPT stick resting ominously in front of me, I realized I knew next to nothing about the actual abortion procedure. Sure, I'd read some magazine articles

> I was in no position emotionally or fi-nancially to take on the responsibility of having a child.

and had seen debates on TV, but it was hardly what I needed to prepare myself. Uncertainties crowded in on me: How much will it hurt? Will we have enough money to pay for it? Can it damage my body? Will I freak out?

At the Clinic

Thankfully, Scott helped me through the worst of the panic. That very same day, he drove me to a women's clinic located two hours from where we lived.

Inside, the clinic looked just like any other doctor's office. Two receptionists sat behind a glass partition. The only glaring difference? The counters were covered with pamphlets about AIDS, STDs [sexually transmitted diseases] and pregnancy. A few plants hung from the ceiling, and a TV in the corner was tuned to Oprah. The women at the front desk were friendly, and they sent me off to a chair with paperwork and a booklet about abortion. To stop the tears I'd been leaking for the past two hours, I started leafing through the pamphlet.

How Most Abortions Are Done

The usual method of early abortion is suction curettage. It is performed from six to 14 weeks after your last period. The procedure takes about 10 minutes.

- The vagina is washed with an antiseptic.
- Usually, a local anesthetic is injected into or near the cervix.
- The opening of the cervix is gradually stretched. One after the other, a series of increasingly thick rods (dilators) are inserted into the opening. The thickest may be the width of a fountain pen.
- After the opening is stretched, a tube is inserted into the uterus. This tube is attached to a suction machine.
- The suction machine is turned on. The uterus is emptied by gentle suction.
- After the suction tube has been removed, a curette (narrow metal loop) may be used to gently scrape the walls of the uterus to be sure that it has been completely emptied.

Planned Parenthood, *Abortion—Commonly Asked Questions*, 1999.

While we waited to see the doctor, Scott tried to reassure me. He kept saying things like, "You're going to be just fine." Although at some level I knew he was trying to be supportive, I couldn't help resenting the unfairness of the situation. After all, I was the one who had to bear the bulk of the burden. For some reason, his attempts to soothe me struck me as nonchalance.

"How do you know?" I fired back at him. "You're not the one about to have an abortion!"

Thankfully, a nurse arrived soon after that and escorted me to an exam room. I fought back tears as the doctor administered the ultrasound test. At first he couldn't find anything, then he pointed to a pea-sized dot on the monitor. I was eight weeks pregnant. Unlike some girls who don't realize they're pregnant until it's too late, I was lucky. The doctor informed me that I was still within the "safe" period for having a low-risk abortion.

Next, I had to go back to the waiting room. My nervousness started coming in waves—just when I thought I was calm, I'd feel frightened all over again. Then, they called me up to the desk where I had to hand over $375. Another nurse led me to a long, narrow room. The red carpeting didn't seem to go with the life-sized forest scene on the picture wallpaper. I remember the room was really hot, and there were no windows.

Explaining the Procedure

A nurse explained what was going to happen if I went through with the abortion. She asked me a lot of questions, sort of like counseling, to ensure that no one was coercing me into terminating my pregnancy. She also tried to answer any questions I had.

At that point, I wasn't worried about the psychological effects an abortion would have on me. I thought the experience would be easier for me to handle than for a lot of other girls. I didn't feel any political or religious distress over my decision to have an abortion—mostly my fears were medical. Because of my plans to pursue a sports career, I was nervous about the consequences it would have on my body. I was irrationally convinced it would hurt terribly, that I'd be weak and sick afterward and that major and unforeseen internal complications would land me in a hospital.

Using a pink plastic model of the female reproductive system, the nurse showed me how the doctor would first inject my cervix with a numbing agent and then insert a tube about the size of a pencil into it. The tube, she explained, would vacuum all the cells and tissue from the womb. Then we went over charts that explained how this procedure was far less traumatic than childbirth and about as life-threatening as having a penicillin shot. She also cautioned me that even though abortion was a safe procedure, it was considered surgery, and my body would need time to do some healing. I would probably experience bleeding similar to my period for about a week or two after.

> Abortion is definitely not my idea of suitable birth control.

Next, she explained, I could either have a sedative by injection or nitrous oxide gas to numb the pain during the surgery. I was more terrified of needles than the actual abortion, so I chose the gas.

A plastic nose mask was placed over my face. Things got fuzzy and floaty. Then I felt a stab of pain. As the suction increased, the pain got worse. Despite the nurse's efforts to console me, I started taking shallow, panicked breaths. I wanted the pain to stop! Finally, the sedative took effect, and I had this vague but overwhelming sensation of sadness. The whole situation was breaking my heart. And then, it was over.

I closed my eyes and just lay there, waiting for a feeling of relief. The cramping started, but I didn't even care. After about half an hour, I was anxious to leave. The nurse checked my blood pressure and temperature and packed me off with menstrual pads and booklets.

I Survived

I napped the rest of the day and part of the next. By day three, I had enough energy to go to work and to even go running. For the first time in weeks, I felt normal. I also felt different emotionally. The thing I'd feared the most had happened, and I had survived.

In retrospect, I wish I'd been more educated, so I could have been spared the terror of ignorance.

That's not to say that I ever want to experience an abortion again. I certainly don't. Abortion is definitely not my idea of suitable birth control. Scott and I thought we were doing the best we could, but unfortunately accidents happen.

I feel lucky that a situation that could have scarred our lives and that of a child's was prevented. And I am grateful I live in a time and place where it was possible, albeit costly, to make my own choice. For too many others, an accidental pregnancy has exacted payments that I feel are much more severe than the price I paid.

Abortion Destroyed My Life

Sally Robinson

Sally Robinson's experiences of having two abortions caused her to become an activist and writer against abortion. She blames her abortions for her later infertility and for emotional problems that resulted in years of destructive habits and relationships. Robinson believes that abortion is murder and that it can have severe repercussions for the mental health of women who abort.

I learned that I was pregnant at the age of eighteen, shortly after moving in with my boyfriend. Feeling scared and insecure, I didn't know how a baby would fit into my future. Upon seeking counsel from friends and family, it seemed logical to consider abortion as an option. After all, I was young, pretty and intelligent. I had my whole life ahead of me.

It was a shock to learn that I was near the 6th month of my pregnancy. This fact certainly complicated matters. It would mean that I would have to have a different, more costly, kind of abortion. With the support of those I valued most, I made a decision. An appointment was set for one week later.

Reprinted from Sally Robinson, "The Choice," *The Post-Abortion Review*, Summer 1998. Reprinted with permission from the author.

The First Abortion

My boyfriend and I arrived at the hospital early one morning in April. After the initial screening I was shown to an examining room where the lethal dose of saline was injected into my womb. Within minutes, I was led to a hospital room where they informed me that I could expect some cramping, a little worse than a normal period, and that it should be all over in about 24 to 48 hours. There was nothing left to do but wait for my body's "natural" ability to expel the unwanted fetus. In other words, give birth to my dead baby. I was instructed to remain in the bed and to call the nurse after I had the baby.

There were six girls in the hospital room all together. At first we had a great time! Talk was abundant as many family members and friends came and went. It was not until the first "birth" that the atmosphere changed. Slowly laughter was replaced with fear and pain, curiosity gave way to sorrow, and a solemn quiet crept over the room. It was in the moments that followed that my life changed forever.

> Without realizing it, the afternoon that they put my baby in a bucket was the beginning of self-hatred.

I'm still surprised at how little physical pain there was. It was similar to having a bowel movement—until I became curious and looked under the covers to see what was there—until that instant when I saw a *baby*, red and bloody and small, but a baby still. I quickly covered myself back up and called the nurse.

While I waited, I became terrified that "it" wasn't dead. Lying in the same bed with me was flesh and blood! The emotions that overwhelmed me in that moment were so strong that my body reacted with violent, uncontrollable shaking. Tears streamed down my face and panic gripped my heart.

It seemed that an eternity passed before the nurse finally came. I watched her calmly close the curtain and put on a pair of plastic gloves. As she lifted up the sheet I turned my head. I couldn't watch as she placed my "waste" in a white paper bucket. As she turned to go, what was left of my childhood went with her, but somehow I managed to close my mind to the events and go on.

The Second Abortion

Two years later my boyfriend and I were married. Within three months I was pregnant again but my husband never knew about it. We were separated at the time and I didn't want him to use the baby as an excuse for us to get back together. The relationship had become physically abusive and I refused to go back.

This time I had a suction abortion. Fortunately, there were not obvious side effects such as excess bleeding or infection. I was in and out of the clinic within a matter of hours. Yet another successful procedure to free me of the awful burden of raising a child. Or so I thought.

I was forced to face the truth of my choices while casually flipping through the channels on television one day. My interest was caught by the picture of a baby in the womb. Little did I know that I was watching the movie "The Silent Scream." Before my very eyes I saw a baby being torn to pieces by a tremendous force of suction. I saw it jerk away from the metal instrument as if he or she felt pain and fear.

In horror, I realized that this was a *living being!* Tears ran down my face as I flashed back to my second abortion. This is what I did to my baby!! Suddenly, the truth hit me and I knew there was no turning back. I had to face what I had done and for the next five years, that's exactly what I did. Through the pain of discovery comes growth and here is what I learned.

Consequences of Abortion

Why, if I felt so horrible about having an abortion the first time, would I do it again? I saw my baby dead before my very eyes, and yet I was able to convince myself that it was okay to get rid of a second child! In total denial, I was able to believe that I had made the right choice for the sole reason that the *truth was intolerable*. The results of my choice were devastating.

Without realizing it, the afternoon that they put my baby in a bucket was the beginning of self-hatred. I lost the value of life. This was evidenced by my divorce and what came after. I became more deeply involved in a destructive lifestyle: sex with many men, drugs and alcohol. Even in the few serious relationships I had, I allowed physical, verbal and sexual abuse because, subconsciously, I believed that I deserved it. Over ten years of destructive habits and relationships were triggered by *one* very bad choice.

The complications of abortion were not limited to emotional and mental anguish. No matter how safe I thought abortion was, I still live with the consequence that I may not be able to have any more children. My doctor has informed me that I have a tremendous amount of scar tissue in my uterus, a direct result of scraping the womb after the babies were removed. In addition to that, two surgeries and many sleepless nights have been spent over a condition called endometriosis. I suspect it is directly related.

> It is *your choice*, but the life you destroy may be your own.

I've experienced abortion and I'm convinced it is murder. Yes, of innocent babes who never get a chance at life. YET IT IS SO MUCH MORE! Abortion not only affects the life of the unborn child, but also the life of the *mother!* I can say from my own experience that a part of ME died each time I gave into my own self-centeredness and exerted my "right to choose."

In my ignorance, I made choices that are irreversible. As a result, I lost a very valuable part of me—self-respect. But I also lost much more. Because of my choice, I learned to neglect an important part of my responsibility as a person: TO VALUE HUMAN LIFE. Two lives were dependent upon me to protect them. Without me, they would have never known life. Because of me, we all learned about *death*.

The Opportunity to Choose Life

To anyone who is thinking of having an abortion, I would say that as I go on living my life, the one I tried so hard to protect from the inconveniences of raising children, I have learned to live with regret. But you don't have to! Today, you have the opportunity to choose life and experience the great privilege that only a woman can know. Yes, others may think that you are too young and immature to handle this responsibility, but *you* are the one who may have to live with the guilt and shame if you choose to end a life instead.

Consider how your choice will affect you now and in the future. Know what the dangers are to your body and your mental health. Find out what your options are if you decide to keep your baby or give it up for adoption. Whatever you do, be sure to consider all the consequences. After all, it is *your choice,* but the life you destroy may be your own.

Chapter 4

Adoption

Adoption Is a Viable Alternative to Abortion or Teen Parenthood

Jeanne Warren Lindsay

For teens who reject abortion and do not feel ready to be a parent, a possible solution to an unwanted pregnancy is to give up the baby for adoption. Less than four percent of pregnant teens choose this option, however. Jeanne Warren Lindsay argues that this is because giving up one's baby can be a painful experience, and that many teen mothers fail to adequately plan ahead in deciding what's best for them and their child. Lindsay profiles some teen mothers and fathers who did choose adoption because they believed it to be the best solution for them, their child, and the adoptive parents. Adoption is an option that should be seriously considered by pregnant teens, she concludes. Lindsay is the author of numerous books on teen pregnancy and parenting, including *Teens Parenting—Your Baby's First Year* and *Teen Dads*.

A couple of generations ago, many pregnant teenagers relinquished (gave up, released, surrendered) their babies for adoption. An unmarried adolescent who became pregnant was

Excerpted from Jeanne Warren Lindsay, *Pregnant? Adoption Is an Option*. Copyright © 1997 Jeanne Warren Lindsay. Reprinted with permission from the author.

often hustled off to Aunt Agatha's home in Missouri where she lived until her baby was born.

Usually the young mother didn't see her baby at all. It was placed for adoption with a family she would never meet, and the entire event was wrapped in secrecy. Her friends were told she was vacationing with Aunt Agatha, and she was urged to forget the whole episode and return to "normal" life as a teen.

This picture changed twenty or thirty years ago. Women of all ages in the United States have a legal right to an abortion during the early months of pregnancy (although in some states, women younger than 18 must have either their parent's permission or the court's approval). Each year about one-third of the million teenage pregnancies end in induced abortion. Another one out of six ends in spontaneous miscarriage.

Very few teens make adoption plans for their babies, less than four percent of the half-million who give birth each year in the United States. There are several reasons that so few pregnant adolescents consider adoption.

First and most important, they, like all pregnant women, bond with their babies before birth. They love their babies just as older mothers do, and adoption is an extremely hard and painful decision to make.

Second, the younger an adolescent is, the less likely she is to make an adoption plan. Developmentally, people in early adolescence find it difficult to look ahead. Getting through the pregnancy may be all she can handle. Trying to figure out what's best for her child and herself for the next 18 years may be almost impossible. Making any kind of plan may require more maturity than she has had a chance to develop.

> Very few teens make adoption plans for their babies.

If you're a teenager, the fact that you're reading this book probably means you're more mature than many other pregnant teens. You *are* concerned about the future—but that doesn't make your decision easy.

Many pregnant teens do not know how much adoption has changed in the past decade. If you think that adoption means giving your baby away to strangers, and you assume you would never see your child again, adoption may seem impossible.

Teens who are more interested in the adoption option are likely to be those who plan an open adoption. They choose the adoptive parents for their child, and they plan to stay in contact with their child.

You'll Get Lots of Advice

If you're a teenager and you're pregnant, you're probably getting lots of advice. Some people feel teens are not mature enough to make big decisions about a baby.

You'll undoubtedly hear, "What do you mean, you'll *keep* that baby? You aren't old enough to be a parent." These people assume that "of course" you'll make an adoption plan.

Probably an adoption plan has *not* been made by a number of young women and their partners because of comments like this. "We'll show them" is sometimes the reaction—along with the feeling that, *at the time,* keeping your baby to rear yourself may be an easier decision to make.

On the other hand, you're probably surrounded by people who can't believe you'd "give your baby away." Your peers who aren't pregnant and who don't have children may remind you that your baby "will be so cute." They may assure you that they'll help with babysitting. "Of course you can manage," they may say.

Some families are convinced that the only responsible answer to too-early pregnancy is adoption. A couple of generations ago, most families felt this way if the young couple was not married. Your family may remind you of the importance of a child having two parents who are married and who live together, parents who can financially support themselves and their child. Your child "should" be with another family who can offer these things, they may say.

Or, and this is the more likely scenario, your family may be appalled at the idea of another family rearing your child. "Not our flesh and blood" is a typical remark.

If a woman is past 20 and living on her own, other people's opinions may add stress to her decision-making efforts. However, she, along with her partner, can usually make her own decision. But if you're a teenager, you may wonder how you'll *ever* make a decision that will please everybody.

The answer, of course, is that you probably can't please everybody. Your biggest concern is your baby. Your next biggest concern needs to be yourself. Somehow, you have to figure out the best plan for you and your baby, then help your friends, and especially your family, understand. You need their support.

Too much advice can make decision-making very hard. After listening to that advice, you and your partner need to make the best decision you possibly can. If you help your family understand *why* you made that decision, they're more likely to be supportive.

> "Placing Joshua was the hardest thing I ever did in my life. It . . . turned my life around and made me a better person."

The decision-making process was difficult. Nick came to me and said, "I'm not ready to be a father. I think we should look at adoption."

I was livid. "How can you say that?" I didn't want to be responsible for any information on adoption because then I'd have to think about it.

I was seven months along when, as I was driving home from church, I started crying. I knew I couldn't keep her. It was a fantasy that I could have this baby and the world be the way I wanted it to be. I went home and told my mom, and we both sat at the kitchen table crying.

Kathleen

As with the less important decisions you make each day, the more you use good judgment and clear-headed thinking to work out your final adoption or parenting plan, the more your family will concur. Perhaps they will realize you *are* mature enough to do what you've decided is best for you and your baby.

Making the Decision

If most pregnant teenagers *choose* to keep their babies to rear themselves, their decision must be respected. It is possible for a young single mother to do a fine job of parenting, especially if she has a good support system within her family.

But is that choice consciously made? Or is becoming a mother often simply acceptance of what seems to be—that if one is pregnant and doesn't get an abortion, one will usually have a baby (true), and therefore raise that baby oneself (not necessarily true)?

Many young women are "successful" mothers. They give their children the care they need, sometimes at great sacrifice to themselves. They love their children deeply. But it is difficult to know who will be a good parent and who will not, whether that parent is single or married, 15 or 25 years old. Some 25-year-old parents neglect their children. And sometimes a 15-year-old does a beautiful job of mothering.

Nita, 15, and Joe, also 15, were shocked at their positive pregnancy test. They figured they would keep their child, but soon after they took Zach home from the hospital they realized they were not ready to parent. Nita explained:

Joe was in denial for a couple of months. I figured I'd have my baby, I'd raise it, and then I'd have my life. But it didn't work out that way.

After Zach was born, I didn't want to hold him. I loved him, but I didn't have that motherly instinct. I was concerned for him, but I really wanted to be a teenager.

I moved in with Joe and his mother so I could go to a school with childcare. Zach and I went back and forth to school on the city bus, but he kept getting sick.

My grandma had always talked to me about adoption. Then I was talking to a counselor at school about my problems, and she said it wasn't too late for adoption. Zach was two months old then. I mentioned it to Joe, and he said he'd been thinking about it, too, but he didn't say anything because he didn't want to upset me.

Birth Fathers and Adoption Planning

What rights should fathers have in adoption planning? What rights *do* fathers have?

Married couples, of course, normally share parental rights. If a married woman wishes to release her baby for adoption, her husband must also sign the legal relinquishment—even if he is not the child's father.

Years ago, an unmarried father's permission was not required if the mother made an adoption plan. Only the mother's signature was needed. Today, however, the father's signature, if he can be found, is almost always required before the adoption can be finalized.

If you are considering an adoption plan, and you aren't with your baby's father, it is extremely important that you know the law in your state or province regarding the father's signature in an adoption. Courts and agencies in most states insist that both parents must consent to the release of their child.

If the father can't be found, agencies usually try to locate him. If they can't find him, the court is petitioned to remove the rights of the absent or unknown father. After a certain period of time, the child can then be released for adoption.

Sometimes a birthmother doesn't want her baby's father even to know she's pregnant. Or she may feel he'd be opposed to the adoption plan. She doesn't want him notified. However, a birthfather may be as concerned about his baby's life as is the birthmother. Shutting the father out of the adoption planning can backfire.

Jeanne Warren Lindsay, *Pregnant? Adoption Is an Option,* 1997.

We decided to go ahead. We talked to an adoption counselor, and we picked out a couple. Three weeks later Zach was gone.

I didn't have regrets but I was very disappointed in myself. I've been through so much in my life, and I always wanted my child to have a mother and father who would always be there, and who wouldn't ever have money problems.

My mom had me when she was 17, and she's right now still trying to get back her wild years.

My mother was very very sad about the adoption, and she had to go to counseling. My brother and sister took it hard. I'm trying to teach my sister that having a baby may look like fun. It looks easy, but it isn't.

Teens tend to think "My baby will love me. I'll dress him up all cute and everybody will love me." But they aren't looking at the late nights, the crying. They aren't thinking, "How am I going to get to the doctor when I can't even drive yet?" I didn't like relying on other people.

Joe commented:

When I finally realized I would be a father, I was all happy. Nita mentioned adoption back then, but I said, "Let's keep it. We can handle it." So I quit going to school, and I got a job.

It didn't work out. We couldn't afford him, and we weren't even living together after she went back home. She and my mom didn't get along.

I started thinking about adoption after Zach was born. He was more expensive than I thought—the diapers, the formula . . . and sometimes I'd miss out on work because I had to watch him.

We were all sad. When I'm in my room by myself, I think about him. It's getting better as time goes by. We're getting pictures of the baby pretty often.

I want to parent when I can afford it, when I have a place of my own—maybe when I'm 30!

Keeping the Pregnancy Secret

Often a young woman keeps her pregnancy secret from everyone for several months:

Nobody knew for several months except the birthfather. I was

16, and I didn't want to accept reality. Then when I finally accepted it, I didn't want to let anybody know because I had let people down.

The birthfather would call and ask what he could do, but I kind of pushed him out, too. I wanted to do this on my own, and I see now that wasn't a good thing.

Finally I let my closest aunt know. She said, "Are you sure?"

I said, "Yes. I sit in class and feel the baby moving." So she came over and told my parents. That was very emotional, the first time I ever saw my father cry.

We found an agency we liked, and that was the best thing that happened. I enrolled there the last 1½ months, and they helped me a lot with information and sorting out my thoughts on what I would do.

During all this time I was alone, I thought, "I'm not ready for this. I don't want my child to come into this world and not have what I have."

I wanted her to have two parents, and I wanted her to have more than I could give. I didn't have a job, and I didn't want to rob her of anything. So I decided adoption was best.

Yvette

If you, like Yvette, are not talking to anyone about your pregnancy, that may be the first thing you need to do. You may be afraid to tell your parents, but over and over, my students have told me how their parents, after an initial outburst, quickly became supportive of their pregnant daughter. Your family may be more supportive than you expect.

Sonia, like so many teens, had a hard time telling her parents she was pregnant. When she finally did, their support became an important part of her decision-making:

I was 16, a junior in high school, and Jake and I had been together about six months. I knew I was pregnant that first month. I went into denial—I didn't tell anybody, not even Jake. I was on the track team, running five miles a day cross-country.

I knew my being pregnant would hurt my parents, and I didn't know how to approach them. I was scared, and I withdrew from them and from all my friends. I didn't want to be around anybody. I wore baggy clothes. The first time I felt him move inside me I just wanted to die.

When I finally told Jake I was pregnant, he was as scared as I was.

> If you don't know much about adoption, one of the best things you can do is find a birthparent . . . or a birthparent support group, and learn about their experiences.

Then one day I woke up and realized this baby was important. Somehow I knew it was not for me, but I needed to take care of it. I told my parents, and they were real upset. I had never seen my dad cry before. My brothers were very upset, too.

After a few days they came around with "We're going to support you in whatever you decide to do." That meant the world to me. I don't think I could have gone through it without my mom.

Placing Joshua was the hardest thing I ever did in my life. It changed my life, turned my life around and made me a better person. If I had it to do over again, I would place him again, even with what I went through with Jake. I live with it every day of my life. Not a day goes by that I don't think of Joshua. His happiness keeps me going.

Talking with Birthmother Helps

Maggie, pregnant at 17, worked part-time in an office with a birthmother who talked about her child's adoption. Otherwise, Maggie might never have considered an adoption plan:

Six years ago I got pregnant, three months before I graduated.

I didn't know anything about adoption—it's not talked about much. But I was lucky to be working with a girl who had gone through an adoption, and I knew about it because she was very open.

If it had not been for her, I might never have thought about adoption.

If you don't know much about adoption, one of the best things you can do is find a birthparent, either an individual or a birthparent support group, and learn about their experiences. Maggie continued:

> *I always thought I would go to college, get married, then have kids, in that order. And I knew I wasn't emotionally ready to parent.*

> *So after this friend and I talked, I called a counselor at an agency. She explained all about adoption and all the different ways to go about it. That's what I liked, the flexibility where you and the adoptive parents make the decisions.*

> *The father was out of the picture because we had broken up. I did tell him, and at first he was supportive. Then a few days later he came over and told me he didn't want to have any more to do with me, no matter what I wanted to do.*

> *I felt I couldn't give my child either the emotional or financial support I had growing up. This was important to me. I was scared, especially as to what people would think of me. I was afraid people would think I was uncaring, and didn't love my child. But I knew that wasn't so.*

> *I tried not to become attached to my baby while I was pregnant, but of course you do.*

> *I had a good support system with my friends and my mother. It was hard to do, and I can't imagine going through it without support.*

How Does Adoption Affect Children?

Do you know adopted children who have known they were adopted, that they are "special," for as long as they can remember? For some birthparents, hearing from adoptees how they feel about adoption helps:

> *They had a program at the maternity home where you could meet people who had adopted. They brought their children to a picnic, and I said I'd babysit. There was a little girl who was three, another seven or eight, and another who was ten, and all three were adopted. They knew much more about adoption than I did.*

> *The youngest little girl asked me, "Are you going to have your baby adopted?"*

I said "What do you know about adoption?"

She said, "I'm adopted and I have two sets of parents. My mommy says I'm more loved because I have four parents." Then she said, "Your baby would be so loved"—this from a three-year-old!

I also got to meet my counselor's two adopted children, a daughter two years older than me, and a son four years older. I told her they were so like her and she said, "You know they are adopted???" And I was thunderstruck because they seemed so happy.

I started thinking more and more about adoption.

Tatum

Having, caring for, and loving children are joyful situations for many people. It is an especially joyful happening if the timing is "right." Parenthood at 17—or even 15—may be right for some people. But postponing parenthood for a few years might make it more joyful for others.

Adoption is an option!

Information on Adoption for Birth Mothers

Debra G. Smith

In adoption circles, a woman who gives up her child for adoption is called a birth mother. Debra G. Smith of the National Adoption Information Clearinghouse (NAIC) describes the types of adoption available and provides other information for prospective birth mothers. Adoptions can be arranged through an agency or privately. In a confidential adoption, the birth parents and adoptive parents never meet, and the birth mother does not remain in contact with the child. In an open adoption, the birth parents and adoptive parents have some level of contact that in some cases continues after the child is adopted. The NAIC was established by Congress in 1987 to provide information to the public on all aspects of adoption.

If you are pregnant and not sure that you want to keep the baby, you might be thinking about adoption.

Pregnancy causes many changes, both physical and emotional. It can be a very confusing time for a woman, even in the best of circumstances. Talking to a counselor about your options might help. But how do you start?

Excerpted from Debra G. Smith, "Are You Pregnant and Thinking About Adoption," an online article found at the National Adoption Information Clearinghouse (www.calib.com/naic/pubs/f_pregna.htm).

This article gives you, the birth mother, information about counseling and adoption. It addresses many questions you might have:

- Who can I talk to about my options?
- Should I place my child for adoption?
- What are the different types of adoption?
- How do I arrange an adoption through an agency?
- How do I arrange a private adoption?
- What if my baby is a child of color?
- How do I arrange for future contact with my child if I want it?

If you want more information on these adoption issues, or any others, please contact the National Adoption Information Clearinghouse at (703) 352-3488 or (888) 251-0075, 330 C Street, SW, Washington, D.C. 20447.

Options

Who Can I Talk to About My Options? If you want to talk to a professional about your options, there are different places you can go. . . .

- *Crisis pregnancy center*—This is a place where they talk only to pregnant women. It might even have a maternity center attached where you could live until the baby is born.
- *Family planning clinic*—This is a place where women get birth control information or pregnancy tests.
- *Adoption agency*—This choice is good if you are already leaning strongly in the direction of adoption.
- *Health department* or *social services*—A food stamps or welfare worker can tell you which clinic or department is the right one.
- *Mental health center* or *family service agency*—Counselors at these places help all kinds of people in all kinds of situations.

No matter where you go for counseling, a counselor should always treat you with respect and make you feel good about yourself. A counselor may have strong feelings about adoption, abortion, and parenting a child. In order to make up your own mind, it is important for you to get clear answers from your counselor to three questions that will help you choose the best option.

- If I feel I cannot carry my pregnancy to term, how will you help me?
- If I decide to take care of my baby myself, how will you help me do that?
- If I want to place my baby for adoption, will you help me find an adoption agency or attorney who will listen to what I think is right for us?

If you are not happy with the answers you get, you may wish to find a counselor at another place. The Clearinghouse can tell you about crisis pregnancy centers and adoption agencies in each State, and can also help you find other counseling agencies in your area.

Should I Place My Child for Adoption? The decision to place a child for adoption is a difficult one. It is an act of great courage and much love. Remember, adoption is permanent. The adoptive parents will raise your child and have legal authority for his or her welfare. You need to think about these questions as you make your decision.

Have I explored all possibilities?

Pregnancy can affect your feelings and emotions. Are you only thinking about adoption because you have money problems, or because your living situation is difficult? These problems might be temporary. Have you called Social Services to see what they can do, or asked friends and family if they can help? If you have done these

> Remember, adoption is permanent.

things and still want adoption, you will feel more content with your decision.

Will the adoptive parents take good care of my child?

Prospective adoptive parents are carefully screened and give a great deal of information about themselves. They are visited in their home several times by a social worker and must provide personal references. They are taught about the special nature of adoptive parenting before an adoption takes place. By the time an agency has approved adoptive parents for placement, they have gotten to know them very well, and feel confident they would make good parents. This does not promise that they will be perfect parents, but usually decent people who really want to care for children.

> There are two types of adoptions, confidential and open.

Will my child wonder why I placed him (or her) for adoption?

Probably. But adoption in the 1990's is probably a lot different from what it was when you were growing up. Most adopted adults realize that their birth parents placed them for adoption out of love, and because it was the best they knew how to do. Hopefully your child will come to realize that a lot of his or her wonderful traits come from you. And if you have an open adoption, it is likely that you will be able to explain to the child why you chose adoption.

Why am I placing my child for adoption?

If your answer is because it is what you, or you and your partner think is best, then it is a good decision. Now it is time to move forward, and not feel guilty.

Types of Adoption

What Are the Different Types of Adoption?

There are two types of adoptions, confidential and open.

Confidential: The birth parents and the adoptive parents never know each other. Adoptive parents are given background information about you and the birth father that they would need to help them take care of the child, such as medical information.

Open: The birth parents and the adoptive parents know something about each other. There are different levels of openness:

• *Least open*—You will read about several possible adoptive families and pick the one that sounds best for your baby. You will not know each other's names.

- *More open*—You and the possible adoptive family will speak on the telephone and exchange first names.
- *Even more open*—You can meet the possible adoptive family. Your social worker or attorney will arrange the meeting at the adoption agency or attorney's office.
- *Most open*—You and the adoptive parents share your full names, addresses, and telephone numbers. You stay in contact with the family and your child over the years, by visiting, calling, or writing each other.

Talk to your counselor about the type of adoption that is best for you. Do you want to help decide who adopts your child? Would you mind if a single person adopted your child, or a couple of a different race than you? Would you like to be able to share medical information with your child's family that may only become known in the future?

If you have strong feelings about these things, work with an agency or attorney who you feel will listen to what you want.

If you do not have strong feelings about these things, the adoption agency or attorney will decide who adopts your child based on who they think can best care for the child.

Public and Private Adoptions

How Do I Arrange an Adoption Through an Agency?

In all States, you can work with a licensed child placing (adoption) agency. In all but four States, you can also work directly with an adopting couple or their attorney without using an agency.

Private adoption agencies arrange most infant adoptions. To find private adoption agencies in your area, either contact The Clearinghouse or look in the yellow pages of your local phone book under "Adoption Agencies."

There are several types of private adoption agencies. Some are for profit and some are nonprofit. Some work with prospective adoptive parents of a particular religious group, though they work with birth parents of all religions.

When you contact adoption agencies, ask the social workers as many questions as you need to ask so that you understand the agencies' rules.

The agency social worker will ask you questions to find out some information about you and the baby's father, such as your medical histories, age, race, physical characteristics, whether you have been to see a doctor since you became pregnant, whether you have been pregnant or given birth before, and whether you smoked cigarettes, took any drugs, or drank any alcohol since you became pregnant. The social worker asks these questions so that the baby can be placed with parents who will be fully able to care for and love the baby, not so that she can turn you down.

> There are some special considerations if your baby is a child of color.

How Do I Arrange a Private Adoption?

An adoption arranged without an adoption agency is called an independent or private adoption. It is legal in all States except Connecticut, Delaware, Massachusetts, and Minnesota. With a private adoption, you need to find an attorney to represent you. Look for an attorney who will not charge you a fee if you decide not to place your baby for adoption. You also need to find adoptive parents. Here's how you find both of these.

To Find an Attorney

Legal Aid—This is a service available in most communities for people who cannot afford a private attorney. Sometimes it is located at a university law school. Note: Some States allow the adopting parents to pay your legal fees, so going to Legal Aid may not be necessary.

State Attorney Association or the *American Academy of Adoption Attorneys*—These groups can refer you to an attorney who handles adoptions in your area. Contact The Clearinghouse for the address and telephone number of your State attorney association. You can contact the American Academy of Adoption Attorneys at P.O. Box 33053, Washington, DC 20033-0053.

To Find Adoptive Parents

Personal Ads—Some newspapers carry personal ads from people seeking to adopt. You call the number in the ad and get to know each other over the telephone. If you think you want to work with the couple, have your attorney call their attorney. The attorneys will work out all the arrangements according to what you and the adoptive parents want and the laws of your State.

> You may . . . wish to make sure that your child can contact you in the future. There are things you can do now to make that happen.

Your Doctor—He or she may know about couples who are seeking a child, and be able to help arrange the adoption.

Adoptive Parent Support Groups—Parents who have already adopted may know other people seeking to adopt. You can find out more about these groups from The Clearinghouse.

National Matching Services—These services help birth parents and adoptive parents find one another. Contact The Clearinghouse for more information.

Of course, personal referrals are always good. Ask friends and family if they know any attorneys or possible adoptive parents.

What If My Baby Is a Child of Color?

There are some special considerations if your baby is a child of color, such as African American, Hispanic, Native American, or biracial.

Some adoption agency workers try almost always to place children of color with a family where at least one of the adoptive parents is the same race as the child. Some believe that a loving family, period, is more important, and that as long as the adoptive parents honor the heritage of the child, that family is okay with them.

If you want to, you can choose which kind of agency you work with and what kind of family your child goes to. Sometimes not a lot of families of color are waiting to adopt. This is because people of color sometimes do not know that there are babies available for adoption, or they may feel uncomfortable about the formal adoption process.

Unfortunately, this means that some agencies may not be as welcoming to you as they could be. They are afraid that they will not find a family for your child right away. Your child might have to be placed in a foster home until a permanent family can be found.

There are some adoption agencies that specialize in finding families for children of color. They work very hard to let people know that children of color are available for adoption. They also try to make the adoption process less confusing and complicated.

Contact The Clearinghouse for the names, addresses and telephone numbers of adoption agencies that specialize in working with families of color, or for all the adoption agencies in your State. This information is free.

Contacting a Relinquished Child

How Do I Arrange for Future Contact with My Child If I Want It?

If you decide on a confidential adoption, you may still wish to make sure that your child can contact you in the future. There are things you can do now to make that happen.

Many people who are adopted as children later want to meet their birth parents. They have to figure out a way to get around State laws that will not allow them to see their own original birth certificates. Because of these problems, many States, and some private national organizations, have set up adoption registries to help people find one another.

A registry works like this: You leave the information about the birth of the child and your address and telephone number. You must keep your address and telephone number current. You can register at any time, even years after the child is born.

When your child is an adult, he or she can call or write this registry. If what the child knows about his or her birth matches what the registry has, the registry will release your current address and telephone number to the child, and you could be contacted.

There is another way to ensure that your child can contact you if he or she wishes. Some adoption agencies and attorneys who arrange private adoptions will hold a letter in their file in which you say why you chose adoption and how to get in touch with you if the child ever wants to. If the agency or attorney that you are working with will not agree to do this, you may wish to work with somebody else.

There are several national organizations that offer ongoing advice and support to birth parents, information about contact and reunion with their children, and many other things. People in these organizations have already gone through what you are going through. They will be very helpful and understanding if you need someone to talk to. These organizations or the staff of The Clearinghouse can refer you to a group near you.

A Pregnant Teen Chooses Adoption

Britanny, as told to Elizabeth Karlsberg

An eighteen-year-old on the verge of giving birth tells her story of how she decided to relinquish her baby for adoption. She rejected abortion because it seemed like murder, and parenthood did not fit in with her plans for the future. She selected and got to meet the adoptive parents and concluded that her baby will have a better life with them.

I knew that having sex meant that I could become pregnant. I just never thought it would happen to me. The father of the baby I'm carrying is the person who was my first boyfriend—during my freshman year. We got together off and on all through high school, but it wasn't until recently—just about nine months ago—that it finally happened. We had sex, and I got pregnant.

No Birth Control

I wasn't using any form of birth control; I never had. I'd heard all the lectures and stuff, but I just kept putting it off. I knew that I should, but I just didn't want to deal with it. I wasn't sure I could talk to anybody about it. I didn't know how to come out and say, "I need birth control."

Now that I'm pregnant, of course, I wish I had used birth con-

Excerpted from "Real Teens, Real Stories," by Britanny, as told to Elizabeth Karlsberg, *Teen*, March 1992. Reprinted with permission from the author.

trol. Maybe I should've thought more about having sex in the first place.

When I first suspected I was pregnant, when my period was really late, I did a home pregnancy test. When it came back positive, I told my mom. She was upset and mad and surprised at first. She asked me, "Why didn't you use birth control?" and everything else a mother would ask you.

At first, I wanted to get an abortion. But the more I thought about it, the more I knew I could never go through with it; I could never just end the life that was forming inside of me. That just seemed like murder to me. So, from that point, I knew that I only had two choices: keep the baby or give it up for adoption.

I was both scared and surprised. I didn't want to tell the baby's father, but I thought I should. When I finally did, he thought I'd planned the whole thing. We haven't talked since I told him. I don't care if he doesn't want to be with me, but at least he could've called to see how I was doing.

I decided that I wanted to keep the baby. But then I realized that I'm only 18, I don't have money, I want to finish school and I want a future.

Choosing Adoption

At the doctor's office, they gave me a pamphlet on adoption. That's when we called an attorney, who facilitates private adoptions where the birth mother chooses adoptive parents for her baby.

Some women, having carried a baby for nine months, might've said, "I don't know if I can give this child up." But I think I realized that my baby would have a better life if it were adopted. The people whom I chose for my baby have been trying for 12 years to have kids. They really, really want a child—and that's just going to make them better parents.

Not many people are familiar with this kind of adoption. The way it works is this: I went to the lawyer's office. They interviewed me, and I filled out papers stating what kind of qualities

I wanted the adoptive parents to have. For example, if I wanted them to be of a certain religion, I could've stated that. But religion wasn't important to me. I just wanted people who were good, caring people, people who weren't prejudiced. It didn't matter if they had a lot of money or not, although I wouldn't have wanted the baby to go to a home where there were financial difficulties.

The couple I chose—and got to meet—were really outgoing. They're athletic, into their health and nutrition, and don't smoke. They're also really into education—that's very important to me.

Thinking of the Baby

People ask me if I feel any connection to the baby. Now that my due date is less than a week away, and it's started kicking more, I really think about having this life inside me. When it kicks, that's when I start feeling emotional about it. I'll get sad, really sad, about giving it up. Then again, I'm happy to make these people, the adoptive parents, happy. I figure that they can give my child a better home than a teenage mother like me could provide—especially without a father. You have to think about the baby's quality of life. I could give the baby as much love as it would ever need, but I couldn't give it the other, practical stuff it also needs.

Before I got pregnant, I always said I would never give a baby of mine up for adoption. But I didn't know you could pick out your own family for the child. This way, I know my baby will be in very good hands. They're supposed to send me pictures and stuff. Also, if the child ever needs medical help that only I could give—say, bone marrow for a life-threatening disease—I put on the questionnaire I filled out that I'd be willing to help.

Before I'd decided on adoption, I thought that no one could ever love this baby as much as I do, but that's not true. I'm an animal lover and take in all the strays I find. I'm a really caring person. But you have to make a distinction, and caring for an animal, though it takes a lot more work than many people realize, it's a lot different than caring for a child. Love is only one component of caring.

I know I'll always wish I could've kept this child. But I think I'm doing the right thing. Some people might say I'm being selfish for giving the baby away. I try to look at it differently. I would like to think that I'm being *less* selfish by giving the child up. I'm trying to think of the baby's needs first. For me to keep this baby, and deny it a better life, would be the selfish thing. Fortunately, I've had more positive reactions than negative ones from people.

I'm scared about after I deliver the baby—when they hand it to me and I look at it for the first time. I can choose either to hand the baby over to the adoptive parents myself, or let them pick it up from the nursery. On one hand, I'd love to see their big smiles when they see the baby for the first time. On the other hand, I know that it would tear me apart.

> I would like to think that I'm being *less* selfish by giving the child up.

Now that I've been pregnant and carried a baby almost nine months, I'd recommend adoption over abortion—especially for the teenage girls who want to keep their babies but don't have the money. It's more fair to give the baby a good life. If I'd had an abortion, I think I would've felt guilty for the rest of my life. I mean, my boyfriend and I, we were taking a risk and it's not fair to make the baby pay the price. I had to face up to what I'd done, not get rid of it as if it'd never happened. I guess sometimes I wish it were that easy, but it's not.

Ideally I wish I hadn't gotten pregnant at all. If you're going to have sex, use protection. And don't have sex unless you talk about what could happen, what you'd do if you got pregnant. I mean, if someone called and asked, "Would you have a baby for me?" as a surrogate mother, I don't think I would. But this is just something that happened, so I'm trying to deal with it in the best, most adult way I can.

A Birth Mother Regrets Her Decision

Mary Medlin

Mary Medlin, a mother now in her forties, was a twenty-year-old college student when she became pregnant. Her parents placed her in a home for unwed mothers where it was assumed that she would give up her baby (a daughter) for adoption. She tells how that decision exacted a heavy emotional price and that having a son later only increased her depression about her first child. Medlin later searched for and found the whereabouts of her daughter, but she and the adoptive parents did not want to see her. Medlin concludes by saying she would recommend abortion or single parenthood over adoption for young pregnant women.

I was so taken aback by the birthfather's response when he found out I was pregnant. He just didn't want to be involved and pretty much said, "It is your problem." When I went home, the big issue with my father was the fact that I wasn't a virgin anymore, rather than I was going to have a child and how we were going to deal with this. The overriding issue for my parents at the time, which seems so strange now, was that nobody find

Excerpted from Mary Medlin, "Mary Medlin," in *Stories of Adoption: Loss and Reunion*, edited by Eric Blau. Copyright © 1993 NewSage Press. Reprinted with permission from NewSage Press.

out. So I went to a Catholic home for unwed mothers near Washington, D.C., where I stayed for five months.

Nuns and Social Workers

At first, I alternated between being terrified of being pregnant and just hoping it would somehow miraculously go away. Once I got there, I didn't mind the place, probably because I was already numb. It was mostly middle-class white women in high school or college, or young black women from inner-city Washington, D.C. A lot of the other young women were very nice. I didn't particularly like the religious aspect of the home, but other than that I thought they were very nice to us. But they very much had their own agenda, which was if you were white, they wanted your kid up for adoption. If you were black, they really didn't care.

When I was at the home for unwed mothers I had to see a social worker for a half an hour, once a week. The social worker mainly wanted to find out the birthfather's background in order to

> The adoption was twenty-two years ago, and . . . I still harbor a lot of resentment.

have all the data possible for matching my child with an adoptive family. I really got in the mode of thinking that I just wanted my child to have the best possible family, which I couldn't provide—and which they kept telling me I couldn't provide. So I highlighted all the things that were great in my family—all the people who were overachievers. I didn't say anything about being Irish Catholic and having a number of alcoholics in the family. I kept hidden the fact that the birthfather had one sibling, his younger brother, who was mentally retarded. Once they found out that the birthfather went to Brown University, it got really ugly in a way. It seemed like the social worker clamped on to me like I was going to have the best baby in the bunch. They addressed my pregnancy with a lot of the "truisms" of Catholicism: that it was wrong to have a child out of marriage and therefore adoption was the best thing I could do for my child. I felt backed into a corner and shamed out of my child. The adoption was twenty-two years ago, and even after quite a few years of therapy, I still harbor a lot of resentment, mostly against people in institutions who think they know what is best for other people.

While I was pregnant, I was physically removed from my family, and the birthfather's parents became my caretakers. There is no doubt in my mind that they really cared a lot about me. There had always been a pretty strong bond between the two families, and the whole time I was at the home for unwed mothers they would take me out two or three times a week. They were at the hospital when I had my daughter. I had to have a cesarean, and when I was coming out of the anesthesia, I heard one of the nurses say to another, "They aren't her parents, they're the parents of the father." The nurses obviously felt like it was somehow disgusting that the birthfather's parents would be there. It was very strange. I felt like I sleepwalked through the whole experience. Most of it was a nightmare, but some parts of it were really nice; seeing my daughter was really nice. I remember the operating room that had these big windows, which I never expected. I looked out and saw this big field of tall grass and this blue, blue sky. I felt really good about my daughter being born and seeing her. I had to be adamant about seeing her because the hospital staff really didn't want me to see her.

Afraid to Assert Myself

Whether or not I could nurse my daughter was never discussed. I almost felt disenfranchised. This sounds stupid to me now, but I was so afraid. I don't know what I was afraid of—perhaps of having done something wrong and being punished? I don't know what it was, but I was so afraid that I didn't even ask really basic questions. I remember thinking that maybe because I wasn't married and the child was illegitimate that maybe legally she didn't belong to me. It was really nebulous, and nobody went out of their way to clear it up.

The birthfather's parents were crazy about the baby. They even talked to the obstetrician about keeping her—either me keeping her and them helping me financially, or them keeping her. The doctor said this would ruin my life. "She has got to get back to her old life or start a new life." I can't even explain what a horrible experience it was. The whole thing just felt so bitter-sweet—to be having my first child, and knowing that I wasn't going to be able to keep the child. Knowing that I was very young but feeling that I could do this if I got some help. Feeling like I had no right to ask my parents to help. I ended up feeling like I couldn't really ask the birthfather's parents to help me keep my daughter because I felt like it would have been an affront to my parents and that would hurt them even more. So I dropped the whole issue.

I stayed at the maternity home for three weeks after the birth. Every day I would go to the nursery and feed the baby her bottle. It just got to be too much of a strain because I knew that I was going to leave. So after a little more than two weeks, I called the birthfather's parents and asked them if they could get me. I felt like I had to leave because I couldn't take it anymore. However, before I left, we had my daughter baptized. I think it was on the same day I left, but I still don't remember. I don't remember that day at all. I guess my mind is just being kind to me.

I stayed in Washington, D.C., for another couple of months, mainly because I didn't want to go home and deal with my parents. Then I went back. When my parents met me at the airport they said, "We have a wonderful surprise for you. We are going to go on our vacation." So we drove to Arizona and saw the Grand Canyon. It was the first time—and the last—I ever saw it. I have this wonderful photograph of me standing in my coat with my long, straight hair, next to my mother. We are looking down into the Grand Canyon, and I remember feeling just like the Grand Canyon—vastly empty. I was thinking about my daughter constantly, and I was almost not aware of the passage of time. I didn't want time to go forward, I wanted it to go back—not back to before I was pregnant, but just back to when I had my daughter so I could be with her. My parents pushed me about returning to college, and I really

> After I had my son, I got horribly depressed about my daughter.

didn't want to do anything. I wanted to be dead, but they pressed me, pressed me, and pressed me. They wanted me to become a useful member of society. I guess they thought I wasn't really good "merchandise" anymore. My parents suggested I go to secretarial school.

I felt like the pregnancy was my fault. However, I never felt ashamed, and that was the big difference between me and my parents. It didn't seem shameful to me. What I had a lot of trouble with at that particular time was that everybody in my generation was saying, "You don't have to get married, you can live together. Free love, do whatever you want." Except nobody wanted to deal with you if you had a child or if you got pregnant. If that happened you were just stupid. So I had trouble fitting in with people who were my contemporaries, and I had trouble fitting in with my parents. I just felt like I didn't fit in anywhere. During that first year and a half, I tried to kill myself twice. In order to fit, or in order just to keep going, I blocked it out.

A New Child Brings Back Memories

Eleven years later when I was pregnant with my son, I felt really good. I thought, "Finally, I have done it the right way, and I am going to get to keep him. This is going to be great." When I had him, I was really happy at first. Then, as he started changing and smiling at me as the weeks went by, it was very hard for me to deal with. Everything about my daughter just flooded back. I was totally in love with my son, Timothy, no doubt about it, but there was a strong resentment in me somehow that he wasn't her. I don't know how to explain it, but there were so many conflicting things going on in my head that it was very hard to deal with Timothy on a daily basis. Looking back on his infancy, I can see that I felt really resentful that not only did I lose my first child and can't remember the day I lost her, but in a lot of ways I lost my second child because I don't remember a lot from when Timothy was small. That's gone too.

> I would never in good conscience be able to recommend giving a child up for adoption.

After I had my son, I got horribly depressed about my daughter. In dealing with that depression I eventually began the search for her. I went back to Washington, D.C., which was the first time I had been back since I had given her up. I went back to the home for unwed mothers because I thought that maybe I could remember the day that I left. But I couldn't. I still don't remember.

When I found my daughter after a year of searching, I contacted her parents, but they didn't want to have too much to do with me. Her parents did write me a long letter and sent me pictures. It was pretty much, "Thank you very, very much for this wonderful, wonderful child. Now will you please, please go away again and never come back?" At the time, my daughter was 11 years old. When she graduated from high school, I sent her a card. I told her I would really like to know where she was going to college, not because I would try to come there and see her if she didn't want to see me, but because I always feel better knowing exactly where she is. It is like knowing where my son Timothy is. I don't understand why people find it so difficult to comprehend that I want to know where my child is. I don't need to know every second of every day, but I would like to know where she lives, what she is doing, and what is important to her. Over the last few years I have gotten worn down trying to keep in contact with her family, or with her. I know that you are always your parents' child, but I think there is a real strong agenda with a lot of adoptive parents that they can't deal with the birthparents because they feel threatened. They don't feel quite sure of the fact that they really are the child's parents.

Practically, I know that there are children that need to be adopted. But if there was government help and help from religious organizations and philanthropies, I think that a lot more women would be able to keep their children. That doesn't seem to be a real agenda in the world we live in. It is a sad thing, but I guess there is always going to be adoption. I would make it so that adoption is open. I would say live with an open adoption, or don't do it, because if you are adopting a child and you lose sight of the fact that this child has other parents, you are not dealing with the child's reality. Sooner or later it is going to hurt the child. I think it is going to hurt the adoptive parents as well because they are dealing with a reality gap too, just like I always have.

Advice on Adoption

If a young pregnant woman came to me and asked my advice, and she was not able to marry, I would say either decide if you want to be a single mother or have an abortion. I would never in good conscience be able to recommend giving a child up for adoption. If you want to get religious about it and think that abortion is a death and that somebody has been killed, then a death is a final thing, and then you go on. With my daughter, I feel like she is being held hostage and it just goes on and on and on. Adoption has cost me too much. It has cost my son, and as far as I know, it has cost my daughter. It has cost my parents. It has cost my family for not having her in our lives. I think that we had a lot of really bad advice, and we were really naive.

I remember my mother always said that her father, who was all Irish and very dogmatic, said, "It isn't whether it is right or wrong, it is whether you can live with the consequences." Somehow I think the consequences should be a little bit more in line with what went down. I don't think having a child means that you should go through the rest of your life paying such a heavy emotional price.

I can't be around people who have adopted children, especially small girls. I have actually broken off friendships because people have adopted children. It is still too painful for me. I was really scared to talk about this because it just brings it all up again. I feel like I am always paying. For what? For caring? It seems like I'm paying a really heavy price for simply being human.

The Joys and Sorrows of Giving Up My Baby

Jennifer Friedhoff

Jennifer Friedhoff was a high school junior when she became pregnant. She chose to carry her baby to term and to
give up the baby (a girl) for adoption. She describes how
she came to her decision, how she met the adoptive parents,
her changing relationship with the baby's father, and how
her own mother, a single parent of three, reacted. Friedhoff
chose an open adoption and kept in contact with the child
and adoptive parents after the birth. Giving up her baby girl
was an emotionally painful experience, she writes, but she
still believes she made the best decision. Friedhoff later attended college and married.

A child is something so precious that it is considered by most
to be a blessing, especially to a couple who cannot bear children. To share the blessing of a child with a couple who desperately wants to be a family is a rewarding and life-changing event.

I will never forget the day when I found out I was going to be
a mother. I knew that I was not ready to raise a child; I had had
a hard enough time passing my driver's test earlier that month. I
also knew that C, the father, was nowhere near prepared to hear

Reprinted from Jennifer Friedhoff, "My Adoption Story," an online article found at
www.angelfire.com/oh/Jenns1Page/adoptstory.html. Reprinted with permission
from the author.

the news, let alone become a father. I knew that this was the last thing my family would expect from good, responsible, Jennifer.

C reacted to the news exactly as I expected he would react. He panicked. He told me that he was not ready for this and said that he needed some time to think about the pregnancy. He told me that he would do his best to be there for me. He also said that we could not raise this child and that he would support me financially for what-

> I did not want to live the life of my mother, marrying and raising three children alone.

ever I chose. He primarily wanted me to have an abortion.

When the time came to sit down and tell my mother, I was terrified. Often when we would fight, I would say "I am not stupid enough to get myself pregnant like you were." Telling her I was pregnant was like admitting defeat. She was so disappointed in what I had done. She was worried about what was going to happen to my life. I had indeed turned out like my mother.

Sorting Out Options

Still, I did not want to live the life of my mother, marrying and raising three children alone. I wanted to go to college and get a good job doing what I loved. I wanted to give that small child inside of me more than I had, more than I could ever provide.

This desire led me to begin to explore other options besides raising the child, because I knew that marriage was not what I wanted to do as a junior in high school. With the help of my family, we were able to sort out what to do. We realized that there were two alternative choices to parenting the baby. I could abort the baby or look into adoption. Well, that was a pretty easy decision on my part. I told C and my mom that I had chosen adoption. They agreed it was a wise choice.

By the time school started, it seemed like everyone in the school knew. Word travels fast in a small school. I was called by the principal to come and discuss my 'situation.' I found out that because I went to a Catholic high school, the policy was that I had to carry the baby to term. When I told her my plans she referred me to a local agency.

The first time I went to see my counselor S, my mom went with me. All my mom and I did was argue. She never went back to a session with me. In the sessions we talked about all kinds of things. But mainly adoption stuff. I was very worried about changing my mind because I thought that I would never see the baby again after the placement. It was then that I

A Journal Entry

Well, Everyone told me to keep a journal to express my emotions. I had J on Monday. She's 3 weeks old tomorrow. I placed her in an adoptive home. B and M are her parents. I miss her so much. It's worse than grieving a death because I know she's out there. I'll get to see her, but it's not the same. I feel so weird. I know I did the right thing, but I feel like I failed as a mother. The reason I placed her was because I couldn't raise her right. What kind of person can't even raise a baby? Reproduction was why God put us on the Earth and I can't even do that right. I just feel like a failure as a mother and as a human being. I also feel like I was being selfish. I did it so I didn't have to stay home all the time and everything. I did it so I could go to school and get on with my life. I also feel like I've lost everything. I've lost my baby; all rights to my baby; I'm losing the father of my baby—C. I've even lost myself. I can't find the old me. I am trying to be normal, but it's too hard! The new me is quiet, angry, and depressed. People don't like those kind of people. I don't like to be that. All I do when I'm alone is cry about J. When can I get on with my life? My hole keeps getting deeper and deeper.

Love,

Jen

Journal of Jennifer Friedhoff, available at www.angelfire.com/oh/Jenns1Page/journal1.html.

was first introduced to open adoption.

Open adoption is a form of adoption where the birth parents and adoptive family maintain contact through letters, videos, and visits. I liked the idea immediately. I did a lot of research on the various facets of adoption and liked it more and more. I talked to C about openness. He took to the idea pretty readily.

The Baby Becomes Real

As time passed and my belly grew with the baby inside of me what was happening became a reality. The first time I felt her move was on Thanksgiving. That was my first realization that there was indeed a small person inside of me. That was so hard. I began to realize how much I loved this child.

From that day on, I talked to and sang to the baby all the time. I was excited about everything. I also knew that in a few months I would have to part with this person. I would never be this close to this child ever again. I began to change my mind. I also slowly became depressed. I was beginning to feel the sacrifice I would have to make.

I had also lost C. He began seeing another girl. I resented him so much because there he was moving on with his life while mine was at a standstill with his child. I began to resent the pregnancy. I also became depressed and angry.

As the due date drew near, C slowly began to come around again. I was happier. The two of us began to look at parent profiles to find the parents we wanted to raise our child. We finally found a couple we both felt would be a good

> My counselor had told me numerous times that I might change my mind about placing the baby in an adoptive home.

choice. They had a son and were good people. They had high Catholic morals and were very active in their church. They were also licensed foster parents so the baby could go directly into their home. The parents could bond with their child immediately.

Meeting the Family

In March C and I met the family and fell in love with them instantly. Everything felt so right. They were such good parents with their son; we knew they would be excellent with a daughter.

I had a C-Section with J and it was the happiest and saddest day of my life. As I lay on the operating table, I heard and saw the most beautiful little person my eyes had ever seen.

> J knows she is adopted, and understands as much as a 3-year-old can.

As the day continued, I began to realize what I had been told all through my pregnancy. My counselor had told me numerous times that I might change my mind about placing the baby in an adoptive home. That day I must have changed my mind every other minute. The reality of having to give up that small, beautiful, and helpless little creature that I had carried in my body for nine months hit me so hard. That night C and I sat as a family with the baby and discussed how real everything had become. We both realized that now, even more, she deserved more than we could ever give her.

When the day came to leave the hospital, I was an emotional mess. That was the first and only time I ever saw C cry. I wanted so badly to take her [the baby] with me, but I could not care for her the way her new parents could. I could also not take away their chance of raising another baby. I went into the hospital as two and left alone.

The papers were signed five days after she was born. The adoption was finalized one year later.

To be honest I don't remember when the contact with B and M began. That whole year was a blur of pain and happiness. The adoption was final on her first birthday. We did have visits during the first year. I even remember one where the birth dad and I baby-sat. The adoptive parents were so supportive through that rough first year.

We have had many visits that usually seem to be monthly.

They don't live far away. So my whole family gets to see her, and spoil her I might add.

J knows she is adopted, and understands as much as a 3-year-old can. She knows she grew in my stomach and that her mommy was chosen to raise her. I find that adorable.

But things are going well now, and I am very happy. I love the open adoption set up. I love the whole experience. The hardest part of it all now is saying good-bye when each visit comes to a close. But I wouldn't trade it for the whole world.

Chapter 5

Parenthood

Financial and Other Responsibilities of Parents

Anna Runkle

Pregnant teens who are considering keeping and raising their children should carefully consider the enormous responsibilities that come with parenthood, writes Anna Runkle. They should act before the birth to explore government welfare and insurance programs and to solicit commitments for help from family members and friends. Many pregnant teenagers have unrealistic ideas about parenting and their future, she notes. However, for some teens, parenthood can bring a new maturity and focus to their lives. Runkle is a former pregnancy counselor and a popular writer and speaker on the subjects of abortion and unintended pregnancy.

The subject of motherhood is so large it would take a whole library to give you all the important information. And if motherhood is your choice, it is strongly suggested that you go to the library rather than relying on this brief chapter. It is also suggested that you get all the help and teaching you can from

Excerpted from Anna Runkle, *In Good Conscience: A Practical, Emotional, and Spiritual Guide to Deciding Whether to Have an Abortion.* Copyright © 1998 Jossey-Bass Inc., Publishers. Reprinted with permission from John Wiley & Sons, Inc.

friends who are parents. This section of the book deals mostly with financial considerations of parenthood, helping you to assess some of the steps you'll need to take to be prepared for the arrival of a baby.

Marriage Versus Single Motherhood

Everybody knows it is a whole lot easier to be a mother when there's another adult in the house to help out. This doesn't necessarily have to be a husband—it can be a boyfriend, girlfriend, parent, or friend. What's important is whether they are committed to your and your baby's support—including earning money, sharing in housework and child care, or being there for you both emotionally. If marriage is what you want from your male partner, now is the time to have that conversation. Marriage does not guarantee that he will support you, however. Again, it is his commitment that counts.

> Now is the time to get commitments from your partner, friends, and relatives about just how much help they will give you.

Without a partner, motherhood is certainly possible but it's very, very hard work, especially during the child's infancy. Half of all single mothers have incomes below the federal poverty line. If you work or go to school, you are going to need some adult support besides day care, period. Even a saint would get crazy from a life of all work and baby care.

If single motherhood is the route you choose, you'll have lots of company. As more and more women choose it (or get there because a marriage ends), the more single parents can stick together (the personal ads in some news weeklies these days even have special sections for single parents who want to meet each other).

Now is the time to get commitments from your partner, friends, and relatives about just how much help they will give you. Can you live with your parents for a while? Will your sister offer to baby-sit once a week? Will your grandfather pay for your health insurance? Will your employer convert your job to a shared position so you can cut down to part-time? Is your partner willing to care for the baby on certain days? You cannot and should not try to do it all by yourself. Don't be afraid to ask for what you need, but be realistic about how well you expect these people to fulfill the commitments they make. . . .

A Parent's Financial Obligations

Child Support Payments. You are entitled to child support payments from your child's father even if he's not working and even if you marry someone else. The average child support payment is about $250 a month, depending on the incomes of the parents. States are passing tougher enforcement laws to get noncustodial parents (the ones who don't have custody) to pay the full amount of their court-ordered support, but most do not. To get child sup-

Costs for Baby's First Year

	Basic Stuff	Nicer Stuff
Diapers	$610	$900
Baby Formula	$500	$600
Baby Food	$200	$300
Baby Care Products (bottles, wipes, lotion)	$150	$225
Baby Clothes & Shoes	$200 (second hand)	$450
Furniture (crib, high chair, car seat, stroller)	$300 (second hand)	$500
Child Care (full-time)	$10,400	$16,000
Medical Expenses	$4,200	$7,500
Housing	$5,400 (1 bedroom)	$7,200 (2 bedrooms)
Utilities	$900	$1,200
Your Expenses (food, clothes, transport)	$3,300	$5,000
Total for One Year:	$26,660	$40,575

Source: Minnesota Organization on Adolescent Pregnancy, Prevention, and Parenting

port payments, you will have to establish that your male partner is in fact the father. If he does not voluntarily admit he is the father, you can initiate a paternity suit. For information about this procedure, call your county district attorney's office.

Child Care. If you work, you will need child care. If this can't be provided for free by a friend or relative, child care will probably be the largest expense associated with your child. Costs vary in different communities throughout the country, but expect to pay about the same amount it would cost to rent a small one-bedroom apartment in your community. Just as rents vary from neighborhood to neighborhood, child care costs vary according to quality and other factors.

> If you are under eighteen and unmarried, you'll have to live with your parents or in some other adult-supervised situation in order to get [welfare].

Long-Term Health Insurance. Having health insurance is extremely important for parents and their children, and it can be very hard to pay for. If you're receiving welfare or not working, you may qualify for Medicaid. Medicaid is the federal health insurance program for low-income families. If you have a low-paying job that does not provide health coverage for you and your dependents, however, you could be in a tough position. Many Americans are stuck between being eligible for Medicaid and being able to afford private health insurance. Unfortunately, there is no easy solution for you if this is your predicament.

Government Funding for Mothers and Children

Government funds are sometimes available for low-income mothers. The recent reform of the welfare system has changed a lot of the rules, but here's the basic information.

- Welfare used to be called AFDC, but now it's called TANF. This stands for "temporary assistance to needy families" and people pronounce it "tanniff."

- Welfare used to come from the U.S. government but now it comes from your state government.
- Your state can make a lot of its own rules about who gets it and how much. For this reason, you should call your county offices to find out if you are eligible and what rules apply.
- Welfare payments average less than $400 a month. Payments vary a lot by state, so it could be a lot less than this.
- You are now required to start working within two years of receiving welfare. Some counties have programs to help you with job training and child care, though these programs are not always very good. Some states will let you go to vocational school for one year instead of working for that year.
- There is now a lifetime limit of five years for receiving welfare. If you get welfare for five years, does this mean the state will let you starve to death? Not necessarily. States may give welfare to certain families for longer periods of time.
- If you are under eighteen and unmarried, you'll have to live with your parents or in some other adult-supervised situation in order to get TANF.
- Food stamps may be available to poor families in addition to TANF. Legal immigrants can no longer get food stamps.
- Medicaid (called MediCal in California) is health insurance for people on TANF. Even if you are no longer eligible for TANF, you may still be eligible for Medicaid.
- States can now take stronger actions to get your male partner to pay child support (but don't count on receiving child support payments).
- All these programs have complicated procedures and paperwork for the people who want them, so get started early on the application process.
- Your doctor or clinic can tell you who to call or visit to get started (Children's Defense Fund). . . .

If You're a Teen

When I counsel pregnant teenagers who are leaning toward parenting, I often find they have unrealistic ideas about babies, their future, and their male partner. "I know my boyfriend's going to be there for me," these girls will typically assure me. "I'm pretty sure we'll get married and have a nice house." The short time period during which girls must decide about their pregnancies is no time for denial and vagueness.

> No matter what your boyfriend says, you should know that relationships between teen mothers and their male partners almost never last.

Eighty percent of teens who have babies drop out of high school. Those who don't usually have strong family support and child care. Most cities have programs that provide child care while teen mothers attend adult school, but completion is rare. If you're thinking about becoming a mom, ask yourself honestly if you have the family support and self-discipline to devote almost all your waking hours to classes, studies, and caring for a baby.

No matter what your boyfriend says, you should know that relationships between teen mothers and their male partners almost never last, no matter how good the relationship is now. Girls should never count on support from their male partner. Precious few even participate financially in the child's life, even though they are required to by law.

Welfare, food stamps, and Medicaid will cover medical and some living expenses for some teens and their children for a lifetime total of five years. With new welfare reform laws, teen mothers must live with their parents or in approved, adult-supervised situations and they must go to high school until they turn eighteen or graduate. All mothers who receive welfare must start working and at least partially support themselves within two years. It is somewhat unlikely when the time is up that you will be able to support yourself and your child without outside support. Family support is essential; commitments from family members should be obtained now, while you still have options about your pregnancy.

Now, with all that negative stuff out of the way, here is the positive side. Many teen mothers say that having a baby was the best thing that ever happened to them. These mothers are comfortable with the hard work required and with the limitations on their social life. Some say having a baby gave them a focus and helped them get their lives together. If having a baby is your choice, and if you're committed enough, you can make your life a success.

The Many Challenges of Parenthood

Gail B. Stewart

Gail B. Stewart, a writer of numerous books for young people, interviewed many teen parents for her book *Teen Parenting*, from which the following is excerpted. She describes some of the emotional, financial, and physical challenges teen parents face. While much of the focus on teen parents is on the mother, Stewart writes that it is important for teen fathers to become involved in raising their children.

Many teenagers say they feel as though their pregnancy lasts forever, that they feel heavy and tired and that they can't remember what it's like *not* to feel that way. They look forward to the birth of the baby, hoping that they will feel better and have more energy. Having a new baby to introduce to family and friends is something they anticipate, too. Recalls Diana, age seventeen,

> I was eager to get to the hospital. I remembered visiting my Aunt Marcia when she had her baby—I was twelve, I think. And it was fun—she had about ten bouquets of flowers around her room, and my uncle was sitting there, real proud. People would come and bring presents for the baby, and it was so cool.

Excerpted from Gail B. Stewart, *Teen Parenting* (San Diego: Lucent Books, 2000). Reprinted with permission.

I wasn't really looking forward to the pain of childbirth—I knew that was supposed to be bad—but the afterwards part I was really looking forward to. I just kept telling myself, after April 12 [her due date] everything will be fine.

However, the reality faced by teens after they give birth is often much different from their expectations. Childbirth is usually painful and difficult, and most mothers are physically and emotionally drained by the time the baby is born.

"I was happy, yeah," remembers one girl. "But I was so out of it. I couldn't believe I didn't even have the energy to keep my eyes open. I don't remember much at all, except my mom telling me that the baby was healthy. I didn't even know it was a girl until the next morning when the nurse brought her in. And by then she was like ten hours old!"

Of course, expectations and reality often don't match. Another teen says she was disappointed in the way the baby looked, and that made her sad. "He was so wrinkly and red-looking," she remembers. "I wanted him to be cute and everything. He just slept and looked like a little shriveled-up old man. I kept thinking, 'How come everyone else got cute babies?'"

Postpartum Depression

The unrealistic expectations that teens have, along with the changes in the balance of their hormones, can result in depression. Sometimes this begins a week or two after delivery, while other teens say they feel sad and alone almost right away. Postpartum depression, as this condition is called, can affect a new mother of any age, but it is often fueled by the unhappiness or stress a teen mother may be feeling before the birth.

"Maybe she's angry that the father didn't come to the hospital to see the baby, or maybe she's afraid of what kind of mother she'll be," says one counselor. "There are so many things that affect a new mom, and teens are often the most vulnerable. And if *they* are feeling vulnerable, they look at the baby, and—goodness! They think, 'I'm supposed to be responsible for this little life?' Without strong family ties or a committed husband or boyfriend, this can be a very lonely time."

Kay, nineteen, says that she wasn't surprised that she felt depressed when her daughter was born, because she had been sad before the birth. Her boyfriend had expressed almost no interest in the idea of a baby, and her parents were less than supportive.

"She was a pretty little baby," says Kay, "but I really didn't have much feeling for her one way or another. I admit it. When she was first born, I said to my mom, 'I don't even love her.' She told me not to worry, that everyone feels that way when they first have a baby. I don't know if she was just saying that to make me feel better, or what. I cried, because it didn't seem right not to love her. . . . I wasn't excited, or happy, or anything. It just seemed like a lot of work.". . .

Crying Babies

Despite all the difficulties, there are many teens who find that a baby is a source of great joy. They enjoy showing the baby off to visitors and family and look forward to taking the baby home from the hospital to begin their lives together.

However, social service workers say that when the teen and her baby get home, they face some of the greatest challenges. Whereas the hospital staff was helpful and willing to assist the teen mother in caring for the newborn baby, life outside the hospital is far different. There are no nurses or aides to bathe the baby or to whisk it back to the nursery after a feeding. And although a teen who is living at home may find eager family volunteers to hold a happy baby, those same volunteers are not as willing at three in the morning when the baby is fussy and crying.

> The reality faced by teens after they give birth is often much different from their expectations.

"You just can't believe how much babies cry," says Samantha, fifteen. "It's funny how on TV when they show babies, they're always laughing and cooing and stuff. They just don't want to stop sometimes, no matter how much you feed them, or how often you change their diaper. It's the part of being a mother I hate the most, listening to her crying."

A New Routine

Whether it is dealing with a fussy baby or getting up during the night (sometimes several times) for feedings, teens learn quickly that life as they knew it before has radically changed. Counselors say that learning to put another person first is a great step toward maturity—but a step that is difficult for many teens to learn, in part because they are going through so many changes that are part of adolescence.

"Teenagers are basically self-absorbed," says one therapist. "That's their very nature; it's what comes with the age. They are pulling away from their own parents, trying to assert their independence in a hundred different ways, and often making a mess of things. That's normal; it's growing up. But you can't be self-absorbed all the time and be a good parent. You've got to be there when the baby needs you, not when you feel like it. And if it means no sleep, then that's that. It's a real growing-up lesson, and a hard one."

Struggles with Parents

Another challenge teen parents are often confronted with is the changing relationship with their own parents. Teen parents—especially those who continue to live at home—often complain that their parents continue to treat them as children. . . .

Sometimes teens feel as though their parents are trying to take over the role of being the baby's caregiver. . . .

On the other hand, many teen parents feel that a lack of help makes their lives more stressful. Some wish their parents would offer to do more, such as baby-sit occasionally so that they could go out in the evening with friends.

Others, frustrated at the lack of "time for themselves" that they had before becoming pregnant, wish that their parents could just take control. One girl finds the $300 per month that her father gives her to be inadequate. Although she admits it is selfish, she is irritated that her mother won't raise the baby, as some of her friends' mothers do, so that she could go back to being a "regular teenager."

> Despite all the difficulties, there are many teens who find that a baby is a source of great joy.

"Some of these girls . . . I'm serious, they were twelve, thirteen, and fourteen years old, and had two kids! . . . But they got lots of help, usually. Their moms or grandmas raise the kids; the girls just keep doing what they've always done. . . . Hey I wish I could go out drinking every night and sleep in until one o'clock the next afternoon. That's the life I wish I had."

No Social Life

With or without parental help, however, most teen parents complain that the social life they once had is gone. Often it's simply a matter of time and energy. Friends who want to go out for an evening movie, for example, don't understand that even if a teen parent has access to a baby-sitter, by evening she's usually exhausted from a long day of parenting.

"I'm up early—at least by six," says one mother. "I'm running around all day taking care of Larissa, going to school from noon till four, and by six I'm done. A lot of times I'm too tired to stay awake for the news at ten.". . .

There is another reason why teen parents often feel so isolated from their former friends: They have little in common. Before the teen became pregnant, her life was probably very similar to that of her friends. She went to school and had a boyfriend. Maybe she played on a school sports team or had a part-time job. But the minute she found out she was pregnant, her life changed. If her boyfriend decided to be supportive and involved, his life changed, too. The kinds of things that before might have seemed interesting and exciting to soon-to-be teen parents now often seem like a part of childhood.

When Jason and Jessica had their baby boy, they noticed a big change in their relationship with friends. Jason admits that he has been disappointed by his friends' lack of interest in what has become the most important part of his life—his infant son.

> We don't have much of anything to talk about now. They're mostly my age, but it's like we're from two different generations. Like, they're not interested that much in Tyler. They don't come out and say anything, but it's just that they look bored when I'll tell them about funny things Tyler does or if he's getting a new tooth or something.
>
> I know that they think it's really strange that I'm a father now. I don't think they really know how to deal with it. . . . [Jessica and I] make a conscious effort not to talk that much about Tyler when we're out with those friends.

Money Is Tight

One of the most difficult things about being a teen parent is the financial burden it places on the teen. If a teen mother lives with her parents and they are willing to shoulder the costs of her and the baby, that's great, say teens. But otherwise, it is a constant battle to make ends meet.

"It's one thing to be hungry yourself," says Debbie, eighteen. "I can go without a real meal—just snacking, you know? But you can't tell a baby, 'Hey, go easy on the Pampers, we're broke.' Or 'Don't drink so much formula.' I mean, I figure that baby didn't ask to be born, it was my decision to have her. So I've got to do right by her, make sure she has enough."

But that is difficult for a single mother. Everything for babies costs money—baby clothes, diapers, formula, a stroller—not to mention rent, food, transportation costs, and other necessities. These things would strain almost any family's budget, so it's no wonder that finances are almost always rated as the number-one worry of teen parents. . . .

Not only is it expensive to raise a child, but it is often trying. Babies and young children need constant attention and close supervision. A teen who has not often been around toddlers might be astonished to realize how big a job such supervision is.

Children naturally test boundaries and are bound to get into mischief. Jamie complains that her three-year-old scribbled crayon marks on a freshly painted bedroom wall. Angie is mad because her son has temper tantrums whenever they are in a grocery store. And Safa is furious because her two-year-old has ruined her VCR by sticking a piece of American cheese inside it. Says one young mother,

> You know, I don't know how anyone has the patience to do this all day. How could someone teach preschool is what I want to know. I mean, ten or fifteen of them at once? No way.
>
> I can't imagine having anything nice again—everything I own either has spit-up milk on it or baby food stains. Or she's taken a marker to it, like my purse here—see that? I don't want to spend no money because it will look like trash tomorrow.

To the Altar?

. . . Many people say that teens today are less willing to take responsibility for their actions—or mistakes—than in years past. Some believe that teen parents should marry. "You married the girl, that's what you did," grumbles one man. "If you got a girl pregnant, you simply made things right and married her. Or her reputation would suffer, and yours would, too. Boys didn't think like they do now, putting themselves first and the girl second."

While it is true that marriage among teen parents was far more common in years past, it is also true that, since their unwed status carries less social stigma than it might have in the past, these mothers would just as soon remain single. Many girls don't see marriage as a solution to their problems.

One girl from Boston says that marrying her boyfriend just to give her two young children a father would be far more work for her, and she's not interested in that at all. "He's a child," she says. "He whines. He expects people to do things for him. He's nasty to me. . . . He likes to sleep and watch TV. . . . The first time I met his father, who just moved up here, he asked, 'Do you want to marry him?' I looked at him and said, 'Why would I want to marry your son?' He said, 'He might grow up if you marry him.' I said, 'I can't take that chance.' No, I would not marry him. He acts like a baby and I have two of my own. I don't need him plus the kids. His mother can keep him."

Fatherhood and Maturity

Some experts are quick to point out that the bad behavior of many teen fathers is a function of immaturity. "They aren't bad people," says counselor Randy Brazil. "They're bad dads, yes, because most of them haven't learned what's necessary for them to become good dads. They don't have the emotional means or the financial means to make them able to understand and accept the responsibility of a child. But it certainly doesn't mean they can't learn.". . .

> One of the most difficult things about being a teen parent is the financial burden it places on the teen.

Counselors such as Randy Brazil maintain that immaturity in teen fathers can be weathered, however, just as it can be for teen mothers. "Boys need to be shown how to be good fathers," he says, "because an awful lot of them haven't had much of a role model. They lack guidance and supervision from their own fathers, and now, as a result of sexual activity, they're going to be fathers themselves. It shouldn't be a big surprise that they are tremendously unprepared."

Teen fathers face severe barriers that make the step from boy to father a difficult one. One barrier is the lack of support teen fathers get from their peers. Although there is strong peer pressure to *have* sex, there is no pressure to take responsibility for the children that result from sexual activity. . . .

Another barrier faced by many teen fathers is the poor relationship they have with the mother of their child. Quite often a girl discovers she is pregnant long after she has stopped seeing the father. In other cases, if a boy has not been emotionally supportive since his girlfriend gave him the news, she may withdraw from him. Knowing that he is disliked makes it difficult to summon the courage to make the first steps toward becoming a real father. . . .

One of the most formidable difficulties for teen fathers is money. By far the majority of teen fathers are completely unprepared to support—or even to help support—a baby.

"People talk about deadbeat dads," says counselor Randy Brazil, "but dead-broke dads is more like it. We're talking about a segment of the population that is either unemployed or underemployed. These are not young men who have lots of prospects, either. Many are still in high school; many have dropped out even before their girlfriends became pregnant. Without that high school diploma, without college, it's no wonder they're on the low end of the economic scale."

Ironically, however, it is money that seems to be the demand made of teen fathers. More and more states are making blood testing mandatory so that a child's true paternity can be established. In these states, once the tests prove who the father is, he can be held accountable financially for child support. In fact, he can even lose his driver's license or have his wages garnished if he fails to pay up. . . .

More to Fatherhood than Money

But finances—or lack of them—should not stand in the way of teen fathers' getting involved with their children, say experts. There are valuable aspects of being a father that have nothing whatsoever to do with money.

"It's a complete myth that outside of a paycheck, teen fathers have nothing to offer," says Randy Brazil. "Social workers and counselors are starting to see that now. We know of lots of ways that teens can bring something very positive to their children. They aren't 'throwaway dads,' as they were once called."

Forming bonds with a young child lays the foundation for that child to have good relationships with adults in the future. By watching a father in day-to-day dealings with other people, a child gradually understands courtesy and respect. For qualities such as honesty and patience, a father is an excellent role model.

"There's no arguing it," says one counselor. "A father's presence in the home is a stabilizing factor. Mothers—no matter how much child support they receive—cannot and should not do it alone."

There are a number of ways that teen fathers can get involved in their children's lives; however, many need help understanding how to begin. This is why some communities are taking steps to ensure that young fathers can learn how to be supportive—not only financially but emotionally and developmentally.

One program that has achieved a great deal of success is Minnesota Early Learning Design (MELD) for Young Dads, which has spread from Minneapolis to many other cities in the United States. Classes at MELD educate young fathers on a number of topics, ranging from birth control options to finding and keeping jobs that would support their new families to the correct way to bathe and diaper an infant.

> Finances—or lack of them—should not stand in the way of teen fathers' getting involved with their children.

The classes are taught by men who were teen fathers themselves; this means that the teachers can relate to what the fathers are feeling or to questions that they might have. Few of those attending the classes have the necessary skills to do much of anything at first, but they learn quickly.

"I have young men of sixteen, seventeen, who are so afraid of the baby's size, about doing anything that might hurt their baby, they're almost terrified to pick it up," says one teacher. "They're scared that the baby's crying means that they're doing something wrong. It's a relief for them to learn that sometimes babies just cry, that a father can be just a guy who holds the baby, walks with it until it falls asleep."

The Importance of Fathers

What is interesting to many men who staff teen parent resource centers is that more than 80 percent of the teen fathers they see have no relationship with their own fathers. Many of them are surprised to realize the importance of a father in a child's life.

"If he hasn't ever really known his father, he doesn't know what a big deal it is," says one teacher. "That sixteen-year-old boy with a little baby may feel totally out of his element now. But you know why we need to start on that boy now? Because in ten years, he's going to be twenty-six, and the father of a ten-year-old. And by then, if the father hasn't gotten involved in some way, that ten-year-old will be just another kid in a fragile family structure who has grown up without a father."

"It takes commitment, it takes a will," he continues. "And it's hard, because you're taking a teenager, who only thinks of himself—that's where he is developmentally—and get him to focus on someone else. Making sure that baby is fed, is warm, is safe. It's a hard job, but these teen fathers can do it. I've seen it happen. And the thing most of these dads say to me is, 'I don't want to be the kind of father I had. I want to be there for my son, or my daughter, because my father was never there for me.'"

Weighing Marriage and Single Parenthood

Kristi Collier

Pregnant teens who decide against both abortion and adoption face the choice of raising their children as single parents or marrying. Kristi Collier, a writer for *Teen* magazine, lays out some questions people should ask themselves in deciding between single and married parenthood.

"At first I couldn't believe I was pregnant. My periods were never regular. . . . I finally went to the doctor when I was four months along. I was embarrassed and shocked. I loved my boyfriend and I thought my parents wouldn't be as mad if we got married. They were still upset, but they said they would support my decision. We got married by a justice of the peace. The only people there were my parents and my boyfriend's mom. It sure wasn't the kind of wedding I had dreamed about. Now, I'm someone's wife and someone's mother."

—Anne, age 18

Marriage

Marriage is an option that hopefully will provide you with a husband who will help you support your child. Unfortunately, the odds aren't on your side. More than 60 percent of teenage cou-

Excerpted from Kristi Collier, "Pregnant, Now What?" *Teen*, April 1996. Reprinted with permission from *Teen*.

ples divorce within five years—and if pregnancy is the reason behind the marriage, the divorce rate increases to 90 percent within six years. Look at it this way: By deciding to have the baby, you've made a full-time commitment to a child for the next 18 years; by deciding to get married on top of it, you've made another commitment—and this one is "for as long as you both shall live." Marriage shouldn't be a snap decision. If you would consider marriage, start off by asking yourself these questions:

- Are you and the father of your baby committed to the thought of living together for the rest of your lives?
- Are you and the father of your baby willing to go to premarital counseling?
- What will your relationship be like when you can no longer go out on dates, but have to stay home to take care of the baby?

> Marriage shouldn't be a snap decision.

- How will the two of you finish your educations?
- How will the family be supported?
- Who will watch the baby while you work or take classes?
- How much family support do you have?
- How well do you relate to kids? How well does he?

"It's not easy. We've had a lot of problems, but we've also had a lot of support. Both of our parents and a lot of people at our church support us. We both talk to our pastor every once in a while. He helps us put things back into perspective."

—*Anne*

Single Parenthood

"Somehow I never thought I could get pregnant. I mean, I was having sex, sure, but most of the time we used condoms or something. It was, like, one time we forgot, and I got pregnant. And all the wishing in the world wasn't going to change things. The father doesn't want anything to do with a baby. He won't even

*return my phone calls. I don't believe in abortion. But I think I
can be a good mom."*

—Heather, age 15

Single parenthood is tough. You've got someone to take care
of—someone who cries a lot, may wake up at 2 a.m., and then
again at 4—and the bulk of the responsi-
bility is on your shoulders. Diapers,
food, toys, clothes, medicine, baby-
sitters . . . all the expenses can add up.

> Single parenthood
> is tough.

Hopefully females who take this route will have supportive family members who will be willing to help out, but remember:
Your parents raised YOU. Their caring-for-a-baby days are over.
This baby will be yours, and relying on your family to raise another child (financially or emotionally) just isn't fair. Here are
some points to consider:

- Only 50 percent of teenage mothers finish high school (10
  percent of mothers under age 16 finish). Teenage mothers
  are more likely to have low-paying jobs or be unemployed.
  If you were to decide to become a single mom—and
  you're mature enough to handle all the work and sacrifices—motherhood can be rewarding. But you would need
  to do a little research and a lot of thinking before you
  could get to that point. Here are some questions worth asking yourself:
- How can you stay in school? What kind of job can you get?
- How will you get medical care for the baby?
- How will you afford food, clothes and rent?
- Will you still be able to pursue your own goals if you're a
  single parent?
- Do you have family and friends who are willing to help
  you?
- What will you do if your baby has special needs, like mental retardation or birth defects?

"Becoming a parent, raising a child, isn't easy. You have to

know what you're getting into. I never see my friends anymore. I work all day, then I go to night school. It's hard, and I miss my old life, but I do love my baby. He brings the joy back when all I want to do is cry. If I had to do it over again, I'd never have gotten pregnant. But I could never give up my child now."

—Lizzy, age 17, mother of a six-month-old son

Two Profiles of Teen Parents

Francesca Delbanco and Heather S. Keets

What is it like to be a teen parent? The following profiles of a teen mother and a teen father provide some answers. In the first part, writer Francesca Delbanco tells the story of Jessica Cezre, a high school senior who takes her two-year-old son, Deshawn, to school with her. Deshawn stays at a day-care center on the school premises. At night, when Cezre is working as a waitress, her parents take care of their grandson. Delbanco writes that Jessica plans to attend college and to marry someday, although she expresses concern that having a child might limit her chances of meeting someone. Writer Heather S. Keets then profiles Billy McKinney, a single teen father who is making an attempt to play an active role in his daughter's life. He tells in his own words how his girlfriend's pregnancy changed his life.

When 18-year-old Jessica Cezre gets ready for school at 7 A.M., she does double duty: two baths, two dressings, two breakfasts. When she leaves for Cambridge Rindge and Latin High School (in Massachusetts), she takes her two-year-old son, Deshawn, with her. While Jessica attends classes like

Reprinted from Francesca Delbanco, "Double Duty," and Heather S. Keets, "It Takes Two," *Seventeen*, April 1998. Reprinted with permission from *Seventeen* (www.seventeen.com).

criminal law, physics and geometry, Deshawn plays with blocks and finger paints in the school's day-care center. And when the bell rings at 2:30 P.M., they go home together.

Against Abortion

Jessica got pregnant when she was in tenth grade. The baby's father, Damien, was her first boyfriend, and neither of them, she recalls, "were too responsible about birth control." Jessica's mom wanted her to have an abortion. She even went ahead and scheduled one, but Jessica changed her mind on the morning of the appointment.

Jessica chose to keep her child—not because she was dying to have a baby, but because she didn't want to have an abortion. "I was scared to have one," she says. "I'd heard complications can happen that make it impossible to have another child. And although I was pro-choice then, having a baby has made me feel totally different." Her friends who have children convinced her that she could raise one herself. "They said it was manageable," she says.

Damien wanted Jessica to keep the child, too. Caught up in the excitement, he even proposed marriage, but Jessica had no illusions about starting a family with her boyfriend. "I knew I didn't want to marry him," Jessica says. They eventually split up a year after Deshawn was born. Damien still sees the baby— usually on the weekends, when Jessica is at work.

> Jessica gets a lot of help with Deshawn from her mom and dad, but even so, life is tough.

In December of her sophomore year, Jessica transferred to Crittenton, a Boston-area youth school for pregnant girls. She was five months along at the time. All of her teachers were mothers themselves, and the environment was very supportive. "I loved it," she remembers. "It really made me interested in school."

But the impending birth of her baby weighed on her mind. "I

was really scared of what the birth would be like," she recalls. "I was mostly scared of the pain." Her labor (the following April) lasted only five hours—a comparatively short time—but it was still exhausting and painful. Jessica had hoped for a girl, but she says when Deshawn was born she was "so happy; the love was just overwhelming."

A Busy Schedule

She didn't return to school for five months. Then she began juggling full-time academics, a part-time job and motherhood. After 2:30 P.M. she tries to do her homework, but she also has to get ready for her waitressing job at Friendly's. She's on the night shift, from 5 P.M. till closing (10 P.M.). Jessica works 30 hours a week—and her mom babysits Deshawn.

Jessica gets a lot of help with Deshawn from her mom and dad, but even so, life is tough. Until Deshawn was eight months old, she logged an average of three hours of sleep a night. In the beginning, Jessica recalls, "I shifted between resenting Deshawn and what he'd done to my life, and totally loving him. There were times throughout

> Jessica did worry that raising a child would limit her chances of meeting someone new.

his first year when I felt like I had to give him up for adoption—it was just so hard. But then I thought I wouldn't be able to live with myself." To improve her own mothering skills, Jessica takes parenting classes at Cambridge Rindge and Latin. She fully expects to have more children one day, *after* she's married.

On that note, Jessica did worry that raising a child would limit her chances of meeting someone new. "You think, No guy's going to be interested in a mother. You imagine spending your life alone, maybe on welfare."

In June, Jessica will graduate on time with her class. When she talks about the future, she's realistic about her responsibilities and excited about her prospects. "I feel like I grew up fast," she says. She's currently dating a coworker at Friendly's; he gets along well with Deshawn and helps her with him when he can.

Jessica hopes to attend Newbury College in the Boston area to study hotel management. She'd like to move out of her parents' house and get her own apartment, but she wants to stay close to home. She's happy with the choices she's made so far and is determined to stay on track with her education—for her own sake *and* for Deshawn's.

* * * * *

After dating for 18 months, Billy proposed to his girlfriend, Kim, on Valentine's Day 1997. He had even made a down payment on a ring. That was the night, he says, Kim, 16, conceived. Engagement aside, Billy and Kim often argued; after one fight, Kim told Billy she didn't want to marry him. He, in turn, got back his deposit on the ring and bought a pager, among other things.

Billy lives with his mother and two younger brothers; his father is deceased. One day he came home from work and found Kim waiting for him—with a pregnancy test. "She looked kinda scared," Billy recalls. "She took the test. After one minute she started screaming, 'Baby! Baby!' I just sat down and put my head in my hands," he says.

Billy's Story

Sitting at a table in his living room in Oak Park, Illinois, Billy talks about fatherhood and the future. (Kim asked not to be quoted.)

"I first asked her out on her birthday. I thought she was the prettiest girl I'd ever seen. So when she was strong with me, I was like, This is cool.

"It was literally a month before we started having sex. We always used protection. Every single time. We used condoms and she tried birth control pills, but she had some kind of reaction [to them] and kept going on and off them. Only once or twice did we experiment without *any* protection.

"We are totally against abortion. It's not [for] us. We wanted to keep the baby but were willing to [give it up] for adoption if we couldn't raise it ourselves.

"I was scared and nervous, but I told my mom that day. And I made Kim tell her dad that day, also. My mom was P.O.'d to the max. But she accepted it sooner, and that made the pregnancy easier.

"At first my girlfriend's father wanted to kill me. He was set

Percent of Births to Unmarried Teenagers by Age: United States, 1950–1996

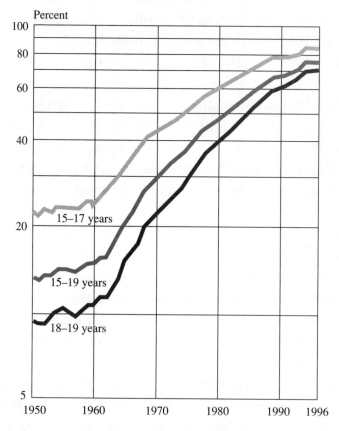

Source: Centers for Disease Control and Prevention/National Center for Health Statistics

on putting me in jail. He used to love me. I helped him paint his garage, but now he totally despises me. He says that I 'knocked up' his daughter.

"Kim says her father kicked her out. He says he didn't, but now she lives here with me.

"I graduated from high school last May. I'm worried because I don't have a job, and my girlfriend's looking for a job, too. I'm at a temp service. So I'm just waiting for them to call me. I might try UPS, the twilight shift.

"My girlfriend called to try to get insurance for the baby, and they said if you're not eighteen, you can't do it. I'm gonna try and call—since I'm eighteen."

After the Baby Is Born

The baby, Dulcinea, was born on November 7, 1997. We spoke with Billy in January [1998].

"The baby is so sweet. She's beautiful, she's growing, and she exercises her lungs a lot. And my mother spoils her—Dulcinea won't even sleep at night unless she's in my mother's bed. And Kim's dad has turned into mush, too. We're on better terms now. On Thanksgiving he dropped Kim and the baby off. I said, 'Happy Thanksgiving' or something, and he said, 'Thank you.'

"I used to go out all the time. Now, whenever I do, my pager is blowing up with messages from Kim saying, 'The baby needs this; the baby needs that' or 'Come home.'

"I'm kind of working with my cousin now. He's a [local] singer. I help with the lighting and sound when he does shows. But I'm not getting paid too well. I also went to this car stereo place and showed them how I installed my own car radio, and they said it looked very professional. I asked if they needed help, so hopefully that'll work out. But we're also on public aid. That paid all our medical bills. And we have WIC [Women, Infants and Children—a nationwide public assistance program that provides food for disadvantaged mothers].

They give us formula and stuff for the baby.

"If I could go back to the day of conception . . . if I thought double-bagging (using two condoms) worked, I would have done that. If I could take it back, I would. But I can't.

"My plan is to do the best that I can. That's all I can do. I want to give my daughter everything I can give her."

Point of Contention: Is Marriage the Best Choice for Teen Parents?

Teen pregnancy rates in the United States during the 1990s were roughly the same as they were in the 1970s. What had increased greatly was the number of pregnant adolescents who chose to forego marriage and become single mothers. Many people believe that the problems associated with teen mothers stem not from their age, but from the fact that they are unmarried and that their children lack an involved father. They believe prospective teen parents should be encouraged to marry; some go so far as to suggest the return of the "shotgun wedding" in which the parents-to-be are compelled by family members and cultural expectations to marry in order to protect the family's good name and legitimize the birth. But others maintain that marriage is not always in the best interests of teen parents, especially if it means the sacrifice of their education. Teens should instead be taught to postpone marriage *and* parenthood until they are ready.

Whether teen parents should be encouraged to marry is debated in the following selections. Maggie Gallagher is a columnist and social researcher affiliated with the Institute for American Values, a family policy research organization. Melissa Ludtke is the author of the study *On Our Own: Unmarried Motherhood in America*.

Teen Parents Should Get Married

Maggie Gallagher

What is the cause of today's teen pregnancy crisis? In absolute terms, the number of teen women having their first child is no larger now than in the early '70s. The big change is not in teens' fertility behavior but in their marital behavior: Today, a single, pregnant teen is three times more likely to pick unwed motherhood over marriage as she was in the early '70s. White teen mothers are only about one-sixth as likely to choose adoption today as they were a generation ago.

Scholars and policy makers have torn their hair out trying to explain these errant young women's inexplicable desire to mother. Are they deformed by a culture of poverty? Are they seduced by a culture of welfare? Are they a product of a nation defining deviancy downward?

A Campaign Against Teen Marriage

To all these explanations I would add, after an intensive study of early, unwed childbearing for *The Age of Unwed Mothers*, . . . a new, overlooked possibility: In preferring unwed motherhood over early marriage, today's young women are not so much rebelling against social norms as obediently conforming to adult advice. The national campaign against teen marriage has been more powerful than the national campaign against teen pregnancy.

And campaign is not too strong a word to describe experts' hostility toward early marriage for pregnant women, despite an extremely limited amount of research on the question. Even today, health textbooks in high schools issue dire warnings that teen marriage "can be disastrous," as a 1996 text put it, transforming teens into "social outcasts."

Not a single current health textbook I reviewed treated marriage as favorably as unwed childbearing (for pregnant teens); no textbook suggested that young pregnant couples who married could use pluck, commitment and social support (as unwed mothers were urged) to overcome the inherent difficulties of young marriage.

How Bad Is Marriage?

Is marriage really a fate worse than unwed motherhood? Probably not. For example, contrary to popular lore, a baby is not such a bad reason for marriage; marriages taken to legitimate a pregnancy are no less stable on average than other marriages. Teen marriages are more likely to fail, but about half of marriages among older teens survive (compared to about 70 percent of marriages in which the bride is at least 23 years old).

Moreover, when young mothers fail to marry the father of their child, they may never marry at all. In one large, national study, unwed mothers were just as likely to want marriage but only half as likely to succeed in getting married as childless young women. These researchers conclude that "it seems women generally are not having children nonmaritally as a response to poor marriage prospect. Rather, having a child outside of marriage appears to derail young women's existing plans."

> The national campaign against teen marriage has been more powerful than the national campaign against teen pregnancy.

Marriage is not a good bet for every pregnant young woman. But by bringing a marriage focus back to teen pregnancy programs, we make it more likely that the next generation of single women will do a variety of useful things: abstain from sex, contracept faithfully, avoid men who aren't good marriage material, and in cases when marriage isn't advisable, consider giving a baby a married home through adoption.

The reason today's young women do less of all these things is intimately related to what adults are saying (and not saying) about teen pregnancy. Why wait to have a baby until another birthday rolls around? Will it really make that big a difference whether you become a single mother at 19 or 20?

To be really effective, a new national campaign will have to abandon the misconception that our problem is primarily "children having children" and work to pass on to the next generation this key idea: Marriage—the gift of loving partner and committed father—is the thing worth waiting for.

Reprinted from Maggie Gallagher, "Campaign Against Teen Marriage," *Conservative Chronicle*, October 6, 1999. Reprinted with permission from Universal Press Syndicate.

Marriage Should Not Be Pushed on Teen Parents

Melissa Ludtke

She was 17 years old, six months pregnant with her second child, and living in public housing in Boston with the 21-year-old man who is the father. She had earned a Graduate Equivalency Degree. Her boyfriend hadn't, nor had he finished high school or secured a job. Did she intend to marry the father of her children?

"Get married? Never," she told me. Like most of the dozens of teen-age mothers I interviewed from 1992 to

1995, this young woman was raised in a poor and fractured family and community. Her mother and father were not married; her mother's first husband was an alcoholic. The second husband, the young woman said, had tried to sexually abuse her. Her mother was unwilling to protect her, she claimed, so at 15, she left home. Soon she became pregnant.

Like most adolescent mothers—and there are half a million new ones each year—she was aimless, failing in school, feeling abandoned. She saw having a baby as giving her someone to belong to and something to be.

> For young parents who have little knowledge of how to raise children well, getting married, by itself, will not solve the difficulties their children face.

Though the rate of births to teen-age mothers has declined significantly since the 1950's, out-of-wedlock births to adolescents are way up: 76 percent of teen-age mothers are not married, compared with 15 percent in 1960. The [1996] welfare law offers a bonus of $20 million apiece to the five states that show the greatest two-year decline in out-of-wedlock births.

Changing Times

There was a time, not very long ago, when it made sense for teen-agers who were about to become parents to get married, even though many such marriages didn't last. Young men who hadn't finished high school could find steady jobs with decent wages, work that provided some benefits for families. There were also fewer expectations for women. If a teen-ager abandoned her education to become a wife and mother—as many did—most people considered that trade-off acceptable.

But today the employment prospects for poorly educated young men are dim. When men can't provide for a family, they are less likely to get married. And when teen-age mothers marry, many end up abandoning their own education. A lot of the young mothers I spoke with told me that if they had married the father of their child, he would have insisted they leave school to devote their full energies to him and the child.

Adolescent mothers often receive essential support from family members—guidance and assistance that enables them to stay in school, learn how to be better parents, and prepare for employment. Some of them would lose that support if they got married and moved out. Also, a young mother's family often views her in a different way once she is married, expecting her and her husband to be self-sufficient.

Marriage and Maturity

Would marriage mean that a poorly educated teen-age mother would read to her children? Not necessarily. Would marriage mean that a very young mother wouldn't become overwhelmed by her responsibilities and harshly discipline her child? No. It is important for a child to have both parents present. But for young parents who have little knowledge of how to raise children well, getting married, by itself, will not solve the difficulties their children face.

Most of the young mothers I visited said they were ready to be mothers, but not wives. They got it half right. Being a wife isn't something an adolescent girl should take on. Our job is to help them, and their boyfriends, understand why they are not ready to be parents, either.

Reprinted from Melissa Ludtke, "Sometimes, One Parent Is Better than Two," *The New York Times*, August 16, 1997. Reprinted with permission.

Organizations and Websites

Campaign for Our Children (CFOC)

120 West Fayette St., Suite 1200, Baltimore, MD 21201
(410) 576-9015
website: www.cfoc.org

The CFOC is a Maryland-based nonprofit organization committed to reducing teen pregnancy. It provides education and media campaign materials that promote the continuation of sexual abstinence among pre–sexually active children. Its website provides information on sexuality and pregnancy for teachers, parents, and teens.

Focus on the Family

Colorado Springs, CO 80995
(719) 531-5181 • fax: (719) 531-3424
website: www.fotf.org

Focus on the Family is an organization that promotes Christian values and strong family ties. It opposes abortion. It publishes *Brio,* a monthly magazine for teenage girls, and *Breakaway* for teenage boys. It also produces the video "Sex, Lies, and . . . the Truth," which discusses the issue of teen sexuality and abstinence.

National Adoption Information Clearinghouse (NAIC)

330 C St. SW, Washington, DC 20447
(703) 352-3488 • fax: (703) 385-3206
e-mail: naic@calib.com • website: www.calib.com/naic/

NAIC distributes publications on all aspects of adoption, including infant adoption, the adoption of children with special needs, and pertinent state and federal laws.

The National Campaign to Prevent Teen Pregnancy
2100 M St. NW, Suite 300, Washington, DC 20037
(202) 261-5591 • fax: (202) 331-7735
website: www.teenpregnancy.org

The National Campaign is a nonprofit, nonpartisan organization founded in 1996 with the goal of reducing the teen pregnancy rate in the United States by one-third between 1996 and 2005. It seeks to raise awareness of the issue and to foster united state and community efforts to prevent teen pregnancies. Its website provides state-by-state teen pregnancy and birth data, tips for teens and parents on preventing pregnancy, and other information.

Planned Parenthood Federation of America
810 Seventh Ave., New York, NY 10019
(212) 541-7800 • fax: (212) 245-1845
e-mail: communications@ppfa.org
website: www.plannedparenthood.org

Planned Parenthood believes that all individuals should have access to comprehensive sexuality education and reproductive choice. It publishes information on pregnancy prevention and abortion on its website.

Websites

Abortion Clinics OnLine (ACOL)
http://gynpages.com

Abortion Clinics OnLine is a directory listing more than two hundred abortion providers in the United States and other countries. The website also includes links to numerous articles on abortion and information on legal and financial assistance for poor women and minors seeking abortions.

AdoptioNetwork

www.adoption.org/bparents

This website provides information for pregnant women who may be considering adoption.

Feminist Women's Health Center (FWHC)

www.fwhc.org

This website for a consortium of abortion and reproductive health clinics in Washington and other states provides information on contraception and abortion and includes a large collection of personal testimonies by women who have experienced unplanned pregnancies.

NOT-2-LATE.com

www.not-2-late.com

This website provides information on emergency contraception—methods of preventing unplanned pregnancy after unprotected sexual intercourse—and includes a directory of providers who prescribe emergency contraceptives. The website is operated by the Office of Population Research at Princeton University.

Sex Etc.

www.sxetc.org

Sex Etc. is an award-winning, teen-produced website and newsletter that answers questions from teens. Written and produced by teens for teens, Sex Etc. talks about love, sex, abstinence, contraception, pregnancy, and other topics.

Teenparents.org

www.teenparents.org

This website provides a selection of fact sheets for teen parents on a variety of topics including adoption, child support, domestic violence, and parental rights.

Teenwire

www.teenwire.org

Created by the Planned Parenthood Federation of America, Teenwire offers a place on the Internet where teens can get information and news about teen sexuality, sexual health, and relationships.

Women and Children First

www.prolife.org/wcf

Women and Children First is a pro-life Internet project created to disseminate information about pro-life issues and to help women who may be in crisis pregnancies or who are in need of post-abortion counseling. The website provides an extensive pro-life resource list, health information, and fact sheets.

Bibliography

Books

Shirley Arthur   *Surviving Teen Pregnancy: Your Choices, Dreams, and Decisions.* Buena Park, CA: Morning Glory Press, 1996.

Eleanor Ayer   *Everything You Need to Know About Teen Fatherhood.* New York: Rosen, 1993.

Lina Barr and   *Teenage Pregnancy: A New Beginning.*
Catherine Monserrat   Albuquerque, NM: New Futures, 1996.

Janet Bode   *Kids Having Kids: People Talk About Teen Pregnancy.* New York: Franklin Watts, 1992.

Paula Edelson   *Straight Talk About Teenage Pregnancy.* New York: Facts On File, 1999.

Arlene Eisenberg   *What to Expect When You're Expecting.*
et al.   New York: Workman, 1996.

Anrenée Englander   *Dear Diary, I'm Pregnant: Teenagers Talk About Their Pregnancy.* Toronto: Annick Press, 1997.

Leslie Foge and   *The Third Choice: A Woman's Guide to*

Gail Mosconi

Placing a Child for Adoption. Berkeley, CA: Creative Arts, 1999.

Susan Kuklin

What Do I Do Now? Talking About Teenage Pregnancy. New York: G.P. Putnam's Sons, 1991.

Jeanne W. Lindsay

Teenage Marriage: Coping with Reality. Buena Park, CA: Morning Glory Press, 1988.

Rebecca A. Maynard, ed.

Kids Having Kids: Economic Costs and Social Consequences of Teen Pregnancy. Washington, DC: Urban Institute Press, 1997.

Gisela Meier

Teenage Pregnancy. North Bellmore, NY: Marshall Cavendish, 1994.

Nada L. Stotland

Abortion: Facts and Feelings: A Handbook for Women and the People Who Care About Them. Washington, DC: American Psychiatric Press, 1998.

Susan Wadia-Ellis

The Adoption Reader: Birthmothers, Adoptive Mothers, and Adopted Daughters Tell Their Stories. Seattle, WA: Seal Press, 1995.

Periodicals

Joyce Arthur

"Psychological Aftereffects of Abortion: The Rest of the Story," *Humanist*, March/April 1997.

Suzanne Chazin — "Teen Pregnancy: Let's Get Real," *Reader's Digest,* September 1996.

Karen De Witt — "Teen Moms Who Beat the Odds," *Essence*, August 1994.

Dari Giles — "Teen Moms: Looking Back After the Fact," *YSB*, May 31, 1994.

Cynthia Hanson — "Mom, I'm Pregnant," *Ladies' Home Journal*, August 1999.

Janine Jackson — "The 'Crisis' of Teen Pregnancy: Girls Pay the Price for Media Distortion," *Extra!* March/April 1994.

Heather King — "One Woman's Journey," *Commonweal*, May 3, 1996.

Rebecca Lanning — "16 and Pregnant," *Teen*, September 1996.

Jeanne Marie Laskas — "Scenes from a Shotgun Marriage," *Good Housekeeping*, September 1999.

Sharon Lerner — "The Truth About Abortion and a Woman's Health," *Glamour*, November 1997.

Marvin Olasky — "Forgotten Choice: Adoption Is a Rebuke to Single-Parenting and Abortion, and the Liberal Media Will Have None of It," *National Review*, March 10, 1997.

William Plummer and   "Revisiting 'The Baby Trap,'" *People*
Anne-Marie O'Neill   *Weekly*, October 11, 1999.

Samantha Rice   "9 Months of Secrecy," *Teen*, December
                      1998.

Wendy Shalit   "Whose Choice? Men's Role in
                      Abortion Decisions," *National Review*,
                      May 18, 1998.

Gary Thomas   "Where True Love Waits," *Christianity
                      Today*, March 1, 1999.

Sue Woodman   "How Teen Pregnancy Has Become a
                      Political Football," *Ms.*,
                      January/February 1995.

Index